China's Highway of Information and
Communication Technology

# China's Highway of Information and Communication Technology

Jiang Yu
and
Richard Li-Hua

First published 2010 by
PALGRAVE MACMILLAN

Palgrave Macmillan in the UK is an imprint of Macmillan Publishers Limited,
registered in England, company number 785998, of Houndmills, Basingstoke,
Hampshire RG21 6XS.

Palgrave Macmillan in the US is a division of St Martin's Press LLC,
175 Fifth Avenue, New York, NY 10010.

Palgrave Macmillan is the global academic imprint of the above companies
and has companies and representatives throughout the world.

Palgrave® and Macmillan® are registered trademarks in the United States,
the United Kingdom, Europe and other countries.

ISBN 978–0–230–55375–0

This book is printed on paper suitable for recycling and made from fully
managed and sustained forest sources. Logging, pulping and manufacturing
processes are expected to conform to the environmental regulations of the
country of origin.

A catalogue record for this book is available from the British Library.

A catalog record for this book is available from the Library of Congress.

10  9  8  7  6  5  4  3  2  1
19  18  17  16  15  14  13  12  11  10

Printed and bound in Great Britain by
CPI Antony Rowe, Chippenham and Eastbourne

# Contents

# List of Tables and Figures

## Tables

## Figures

# Preface

The great success of China as a market economy with distinctive Chinese characteristics has attracted world attention. China's ever-growing economy has made it the economic engine of the world. In the current financial crisis and the global economic downturn, the Chinese economy has been seriously affected but it remains under control. The "China phenomenon" is changing the knowledge balance of the world. Many countries, in particular in the West, are carefully following the development and change of China's technology system and innovation policy. China's leaders wish to see the country transformed into an innovation-oriented society in the not too distant future. The ambition is to become "an innovation-oriented country" by 2020 and "world's leading science power" by 2050.

There has been much debate as to whether China's strategy of obtaining technology by sacrificing its market has partly failed, and now Chinese enterprises are becoming less reliant on foreign technology. As a matter of fact, technology transfer between developed and developing countries possesses strategic significance in science and technology capacity building. However, developing countries, such as China, have to understand explicitly that "real core technologies cannot be purchased but can only be achieved by developing indigenous innovation" (Hu Jintao, President of China and Communist Party General Secretary). Therefore there is a growing need to consolidate technological capacity building and to develop strategies for technological innovation.

China's increased prominence in international and regional science and technology affairs has created a growing need for a deeper and more sophisticated understanding of the structure, operation and performance of China's science and technology system. A broad range of policies and programmes has been put in place over the last two decades to initiate major improvements in the country's innovation system. China's leaders have made indigenous innovation a cornerstone of the country's future development. Many indicators and statistics, such as the number of science and engineering papers that Chinese researchers publish in international journals, the amount of investment made in research and development (R&D) and the number of patents, indicate that China's science and technology capacities have been developing quickly. Meanwhile, China's research environment has often been criticized as detrimental to individual creativity and too politically charged; science and technology policy makers have been regarded as overbearing; and researchers in China face numerous hurdles. It should be noted that the education system in China is largely based on rote learning, and students tend not to be critical thinkers, in contrast to the Western educational system, where students are encouraged to challenge their teachers and develop independent thinking. Nor is the Chinese tradition of deferring to authority conducive to innovation. Under these circumstances, how realistic is the country's ambition of becoming an innovative society by 2020?

China is currently second only to the US in GDP as expressed in purchasing power parity (PPP). China's remarkable global economic impact provides outstanding and interesting examples of innovation. How could a small village like Shenzhen become a large prosperous city of 10 million people? How could local collective owned firms become global competitors in a mere 30 years? How could local Chinese firms, such as Haier and Lenovo, become world famous brands in such a short space of time? Some observers believe that these remarkable achievements can only occur in China, as a result of the radical economic reform and the combination of Chinese characteristics and entrepreneurial spirit.

During the writing of this book, we heard a piece of surprisingly good news. On 20 June 2008, President Hu Jintao, General Secretary of the Communist Party of China (CPC) Central Committee, visited the *People's Daily* on the occasion of the 60th anniversary of its foundation. At *People's Daily Online*, after listening to a brief introduction about the *Qiangguo* (Strong China) Forum, he began to chat online with netizens. In reply to the question "Do you review many suggestions and proposals from netizens on the web?", Hu Jintao stated that he paid great attention to suggestions and advice from netizens. The web is an important channel for the expression both of public concerns and of public wisdom. This is the first time that a Chinese President has had conversations with netizens, and it has significant connotations for China's ICT technology strategy.

China's ambition of becoming "an innovation-oriented country" by 2020 is not merely part of the nation's long-term strategic plan.

There has been an increasing number of policy initiatives geared towards the development of science and technology. China's science and technology prowess is expanding, underpinned by the national network of science and technology (S&T) research of 5,400 national governmental institutions, 3,400 university-affiliated research institutions, 13,000 research institutions operated by large state enterprises, and 41,000 nongovernmental research-oriented enterprises. According to the Chinese government's plan, R&D budgets are to increase substantially. By 2010, China's R&D investment will account for 2% of GDP, compared to 1.34% in 2005. By 2020, the figure will be increased to 2.5%. If realized, this significant investment would put China on a same level with several countries of the Organization of Economic Cooperation and Development (OECD) China would surpass the European Union in R&D investment intensity. Our story of China's ICT development clearly demonstrates that an appropriate and effective science and technology (S&T) strategy will play a vital role in China's S&T capacity building.

## Western management *versus* Chinese philosophy: a 21st century perspective

The preface of this book was written between the credit crunch in July and the downfall of the banking giants of Wall Street in October, 2008. The economic downturn which began in America has affected the whole world to an unprecedented extent. World leaders have met frequently in search of solutions, but the critical questions remain unanswered. The success of 30 years of economic reform with Chinese characteristics has attracted considerable attention throughout the world. China's legacy remains remarkable. The whole world is looking at China. Could China save the world?

In principle in management we are in a position to tackle twenty-first-century problems with twentieth-century methods. Management is an activity with a well established history of theories and practice. Although many modern theories of management were developed in the nineteenth and twentieth centuries, Western management literature notes that, *The Art of War*, written by Chinese general Sun Tzu around 2500 years ago, had a very important conceptual influence on management. Young people from China are encouraged to obtain a Western management degree, while Chinese business executives are changing the international business model. We would argue that it is important that we have the integration of both Western management knowledge and Chinese management philosophy.

We would do well to remember that in the 1950s American-style management prevailed across the world, and in the 1970s, Japanese-style management, which had created amazing economic wonders, became prevalent as the most popular in the world. How did Japanese-style management become known? The answer is that it would not have become known without the wonder of Japanese economic development in the 1970s and 1980s. Chinese management is now under scrutiny. It emerged in the 1980s, after the economic reforms which had started in the late 1970s, and with Chinese business growing from national to global markets. It has been interesting to compare American-style management and Chinese-style management. American management embodies the process of self-actualisation, focusing on "management by objectives" and "management by result". Chinese management, however, concentrates on the philosophy of "self-discipline first, then manage people" in accordance with Confucian philosophy. With the current strong influence of government's central involvement in technological and business development, the character and effectiveness of Chinese management is yet to be fully appreciated.

There is no doubt that Chinese management will have an important position in the management field in the twenty-first century. However, this does not mean that Western management will be replaced by Chinese management. There is also little doubt that the twenty-first century is the century of those who are armed with Western management knowledge but in the meantime it may have to be modified by emerging Chinese management philosophy (Li-Hua and Khalil, 2006). The recent success of the Chinese economy is forcing a new look into strategies of managing of technological resources in the twenty-first century. It is an era when people may need to understand Chinese philosophy and Western management science and may need to integrate Chinese management wisdom and Western management ideology.

# 1
# Introduction

## Emerging ICT superpower in the world

After a dozen years of industrialization behind closed doors, many big developing countries opened their domestic markets to the outside world in the 1960s or 1970s. Since then, the indigenous industries have faced serious global challenges in their home market, and some of them have responded by building up their own core capabilities in order to survive in the globally competitive environment. For these nations, it is absolutely necessary to build up their national business strengths by developing their local industrial champions and exploiting the innovation potential of the indigenous industries.

In recent decades, the mobile telecommunication and internet industries have both grown explosively. As the entire world is now well into the "information age", the storing, retrieving, manipulating, transmitting or receiving of information electronically in a digital form has become critical for the development of society and the economy. ICT is having an increasing impact not only on the people's daily lives, but also on the way business is conducted in China. ICT here refers to any communication device or application, including radio, television, cellular phones, computer and network hardware and software, satellite systems and so on, as well as the various associated services and applications. Technology is an important factor impacting the general process of communications transformation in the world. The monopoly of the old world order was based on analogue network technologies. From the 1980s to late 1990s, the communications market moved from monopoly to competition.

In this period, digitalization was the characteristic of technological innovation. Recently, technological convergence around the internet has a great effect on the market in very practical ways in countries at every level of economic development and market size (Fransman, 2002; Lal & Strachan, 2004).

Recognizing the significance of keeping up with the rapid population of information technology and innovations in the world, the development of the ICT industry has been given the highest priority in most countries. The combination of telecommunications deregulation, an exponential increase in internet and the popularity of mobile information services has created tremendous growth in the worldwide communications industry. The wider application of digital technology will help individuals, businesses and organizations access necessary information.

As an emerging economic superpower, China enjoys the edge by virtue of its 1.3 billion population, the great market this population represents, and the creative potential of its scientific and engineering manpower. China has not only emerged as a major player in terms of consumption of information and communication technology (ICT) equipment, but is also one of the world's largest producers of such products. In the global context, China's ICT industry has established international competitiveness in several sectors like telecom systems, handsets, personal computers (PCs) and some consumer electronics products. China's entry into the World Trade Organization (WTO) has changed the global business landscape which presents both opportunities and challenges to the broader international community. Now China has simultaneously emerged as a major centre of both demand and supply, particularly of telecoms equipment and consumer electronics.

This brings us to the importance of the quality of strategic direction to be provided by state agencies if a late-starting developing country were to become an important manufacturer of high technology products. The traditional image of China as a producer of low-quality and mass-manufactured products remains, but its increasing advances in some hi-tech industries, especially in ICT sectors, are changing this image. This industry has also achieved sustained development over the past few years despite the sluggish development of the global telecommunications market. For example, mobile communication in China has touched a broader spectrum of society, from urban businesspeople to middle-class families and youths, as well as people in rural areas.

China's entry into the WTO has increased the transparency and predictability of the business environment and the legal system with regard to the protection of intellectual property rights in this country. ICT is thus an example of an industry in which the Chinese are able to compete in world markets not only based on the country's possession of cheap labour but also on their innovation prowess. China is also unique in the developing world in owning several emerging global ICT firms. At the enterprise level there are several successful cases in the service and manufacturing sectors. In the service sector, China Mobile has become the biggest mobile telecom operator in the world in terms of subscriber numbers. For example, Legend, now known as Lenovo, which was established in Beijing in 1984, purchased the PC department of IBM with US$1.25 billion and moved its global headquarters from Beijing to New York in 2005. This has enabled Lenovo to become the third world's largest provider of PCs after Dell and HP in the US and increase its market share by the combination of IBM's global marketing channels and networks. However, Lenovo will be presented with challenges such as whether the original customers of IBM continue to trust Lenovo and how the ten thousand foreign employees and the original Chinese employees respond to the strategic vision and configuration of the company. Huawei, a telecommunications company, outperformed Ericsson in the Netherlands with an overseas income of US$22 billion and achieved its target position in the international market. This has enabled Huawei to be among the world's top 50 telecommunication enterprises with business coverage in ninety countries. The third case, Haier Group, the Chinese electronic giant based in Qingdao, attempted a takeover of Maytag, the US microwave oven and vacuum cleaner conglomerate in the Western market.

## Cooperation focus between the Western world and China

In February 2006, the State Council presented its plan to strengthen China's scientific and technological (S&T) progress in the coming fifteen years. The announcement of this plan was eagerly awaited both within and outside China for several reasons. This announcement marks not only China's first long-term plan in the new century but also the first it has presented since becoming a member of the WTO. For the international community, the plan indicates how China aims to strengthen its future industrial and technical development – undoubtedly having a profound impact on the rest of the world.

The ICT industry is therefore logically playing a more and more central role in today's China. In just a few years, China has become the country offering the most attractive market prospects in the world for most ICT products and services, thus making ICT a key focus for S&T cooperation between the Western world and China.

Winning market share or establishing key market position in China have become the important elements in the global strategy of most multinational firms. Many multinational corporations (MNCs) have built their China centers as local headquarters to consolidate common functions and integrate various nationwide sub-units, which will improve their global operation efficiency by consolidating functions, besides manufacturing, like promotion and distribution, new investments and project development, public relations with the business community, public relations with government, training and personnel management.

However, the uncertainties and ambiguities prevalent in the Chinese business environment are neither well understood nor effectively negotiated by the international community. These emerging technologies, especially in the area of information and communications technologies, enable the development of global production networks characterized by outsourcing, the de-verticalisation of corporate structure and new forms of "technological fusion" in which disparate technologies are brought together to achieve the new attractive products that exhibit novel performance characteristics and functionality.

## Role of the ICT industry in the national economy

Globalization has enabled and speeded up the industry's evolution. The Chinese economy has made impressive achievements in building a national information and communications infrastructure and widespread adoption of IT, particularly wireless phones and related telecommunications products. The new technology regime has been extremely successful in the development of electronics manufacturing capabilities, where relationships between domestic firms and overseas investors – particularly from Taiwan and Hong Kong – have contributed to rapid development of the domestic capacity for low-cost manufacture of computers, consumer electronics and communications equipment.

Traditionally, the ICT industry could be categorized into two macro sectors, manufacturing and service provision. Given its size, global economic importance and growing technological capabilities, China understandably wishes to play an increasingly important role in ICT arenas both in manufacturing and service sectors. In 1993, China formally launched the China National Information Infrastructure (CNII) project.

## Pillar industry in the national economy

The information technology industry is a new area of growth in the national economy. During the period 2000–2005, the information industry continued to grow at a rate of three times the rate of growth of the national economy. In 2005, the value added accounted for more than 7% of GDP, of which telecommunications were 4.7%, and electronic products 2.5%. The information industry will continue to make a direct contribution and there will also be a steady increase in indirect contribution. In 2005, electronics and IT products accounted for 30% of the total volume of exports (MII, 2006), and they are expected to become increasingly strong performers in the national export sector. It is evident that the information industry has become the economy's leading industry, emerging as the largest industry in China.

## Strategic industry fundamental to national security

The information technology industry has become the strategic industry in many countries for the establishment of technological, economic and defensive capacity in the globalized world. There is no doubt that the telecommunications network is the infrastructure of the national economy of China. Network and information security is an important area in national security. The strong electronic and IT manufacturing industry and software industry are fundamental to network and information. Information technology and related equipment and software are also vital for modernizing national defense capability.

## Driving force for innovation

The development of the information industry has become the powerful engine of the economic growth of China. The high-tech information and communications industry is the main force fostering the advancement of other emerging high-tech industries. The continuous expansion of the information industry and its constant integration into other economic sectors will create new growth areas for China. The extensive use of information technology will enhance the innovation capability and technological capacity building of the country.

### Core industry underlying informatization and new economic growth patterns

The popularity of information technology and extensive use of information products is transforming social life and lifestyles. Development in the information industry will speed up the progress of informatization in other industries and therefore enhance their efficiency, largely reducing the consumption of resources and transaction costs. The communications network and information technology equipment are the main force and the basic resource for national informatization. This can stimulate and enhance economic growth towards economizing resources, protecting the environment and the continuous development of content-intensive industries, raising living standards and modifying working methods and environment.

## China for 2010 and beyond

China's entry into the WTO will change the international business landscape in an economy that the world is counting on for growth in the coming years, which presents both opportunities and challenges to other business community in the world. However, the uncertainties and ambiguities prevalent in the Chinese business environment, in particular in the area of creating competition and strategic flexibility in the Chinese context, are neither well understood nor effectively negotiated. In addition, the complexities of understanding the Chinese philosophy and local management style have led to anxieties and hesitation on the part of foreign operators, to whom China's business environment continues to present many pressing challenges, particularly in how to manage effective business networks and ensure smooth knowledge transfer, especially in international joint venture projects. In the meantime, Chinese investors are facing even more fierce competition, both the internal and external business environments presenting them with a double-edged sword.

The eleventh Five-Year Guidelines (2006–2010) for National Economic and Social Development adopted by the Fifth Plenum of the sixteenth Communist Party of China (CPC) Central Committee put forward many new thoughts, new ideas and new moves. This will definitely exert a major impact on China's economic and social development, enhancing independent innovative capability as the strategic basic point of scientific and technological development. It will be a key link in adjusting the industrial structure and changing the mode of future economic growth, greatly improving innovative capability, integration capability and the capacity for introduction, assimilation and digestion of new technology.

Recognizing the strategic significance of keeping up with the rapid population of information technology and innovations in today's world, China hopes to effectively integrate the digitalized communication technology by developing her own proprietary technology and stimulate the sustainable socio-economic development in the future. Actually, enhancing independent innovative capability requires: first, accelerating the establishment of a technological innovative system that takes enterprise as the mainstay and market as the guide and features the integration of production, emulation and research; second, improving the market mechanism for technical innovation; third, implementing policy measures related to finance, taxation, banking and government procurement in support of independent innovation, and perfecting an incentive mechanism for independent innovation; fourth, making proper use of global resources of science and technology; and fifth, strengthening protection of intellectual property rights (IPR). These advancements are in line with China's leaders' clearly stated goal to make China an "innovation-oriented country" by 2020 and a "world's leading science power" by 2050 (*People's Daily*, 2006). To reach these ambitious targets, China's strategic initiatives include establishing standards for third-generation mobile telephony (TD-SCDMA), product tracking and remote identification (RFID), digital audio-video coding and decoding (AVS), the formats of audio-video disc players (EVD) and digital home networking and next-generation internet protocols.

## Significance for study

China today is the third largest country market worldwide. It has become the mobile giant, with the biggest number of mobile users in the world since July 2001. China is already the world's largest mobile phone market and second largest telecommunications system market. During 2001–2002, China invested $31.7 billon in mobile telecommunications network infrastructure. In 2003 China's semiconductor market reached $25 billion, with annual growth rates ranging from 15–20%. By the beginning of 2006, the number of mobile subscribers exceeded 400 million. Such a great market potential attracted MNCs from Western countries to join the fierce competition and product development activities. The ICT industry has taken off like a rocket since the middle of the 1990s.

However, since 2000, the abrupt slowdown in capital spending on networking equipment has resulted in massive corporate restructuring and workforce realignment in the telecommunications industry. On the other hand, we note that China has still achieved the sustained development over the past few years despite the sluggish development of the global telecommunications market. It can also be seen that China's manufacturing firms established in local markets like Lenovo, Huawei, TCL and ZTE are now eagerly trying to internationalize their operation and make the most of their ample capacities and resources. The near future will see the targeting of Western countries and the subsequent internationalization of a number of these companies, which, regardless of their success or failure, will drastically change the existing business conditions for Western companies.

China also provides a very interesting case study of the social and technological construction of the national strategy for a large-scale information and communications industry transformation. Accompanied by the industrial deregulation process, the exponential increase in internet IP applications and the popularity of mobile voice and data services has created tremendous growth in the information and communications industry for several years. For example, deregulation permitted cable operators to offer voice service within their cable networks, which pressured incumbent telephony operators to upgrade their copper twisted pair network infrastructure to support the broadband access services. Deregulation also created an open and competitive environment for telecom equipment vendors and service operators both from developed and developing worlds.

With accession into the WTO, China has come to realise that the fierce global technological challenges ahead would intensify. China has recently become a major global producer of information-related equipment and products, including mobile handsets, notebook computers, motherboards, optical disc drives and communication systems. But although many of these products themselves may be considered high-tech, the manufacturing processes involved in producing them are not. As a big emerging economic power, China is seeking to establish and utilize its growing technological capabilities and market power to develop technical standards to approach the technological frontiers and enhance the competitiveness of Chinese firms.

Furthermore, security and image concerns have shaped China's thinking about core competences in information infrastructure and have often been connected with dissatisfaction with domination by foreign multinationals. According to the "Eleventh Five-Year Plan (2006–2010) of Information Industry", approved by the State Council, China will become an information society with a large scale and technologically advanced national information infrastructure by 2010. Undoubtedly China, with its great potential market, hopes to play a more proactive and significant role in the ICT area in future, with its great potential market.

The evolution of China's ICT appears to be a multi-stage industrial development process with fierce globalized competition and frequent policy intervention. The great potential and the booming of China's ICT sector has attracted many MNCs to explore the emerging market. The more recent and fairly abrupt slowdown, particularly in capital spending on networking equipment, has resulted in massive corporate restructuring and workforce realignment in the telecommunications industry. These global giants are eager to seek China, the biggest developing country, as the new growing base for their global market performances.

However, there is not much deep research and empirical investigation of this strategic sector in China. The lack of holistic empirical evidence in this area has limited our understanding of this important phenomenon in the global context. On the other hand, not all international involvement with China has been successful. Many of the difficulties and disappointments are the direct result of misunderstandings, cultural differences or false assumptions, which could have been avoided or alleviated by great care from the overseas partners. International collaboration and knowledge transfer in this emerging country was not appropriately attended to. Furthermore, deep understanding of regulatory and legislative structures in China's high-tech sectors is badly needed by Western academics and practitioners. This interesting phenomenon could be described by a Chinese proverb as "you can not see the real face of Mountain Lushan as you are in the mountain" (a famous poem by Dufu).

There are still many uncertainties in future development owing to frequent policy interventions and decision mechanisms in this big emerging country. And the ICT industry has to resolve the trade-offs between alternative technical choices of the next generation of ICT systems from the political, social and community perspectives. Furthermore, China hopes to catch the opportunity of emerging digital communication technology by developing its own infrastructure system to stimulate its sustainable socio-economic development.

Given that many developed nations such as the US, Japan and European Union (EU) countries have gained strong footholds in the information and communications networks via standards and intellectual property development, the Chinese government now has a strong strategic intention of gaining economic advantage by leveraging its tremendous market size and defining technology standards or platforms in the domestic and global market. Having the ability to control technology standards in the global telecommunications arena will enhance not only the domestic producers' opportunity to develop new products and create emerging markets but also the international prestige of China's high technology industries.

However, radical innovation at the fundamental design level is an integrated process across the value chain which requires policy makers and indigenous latecomers to be aware of the innovation paradigm shift in order to meet the great challenge. With close examination of the footprint of how China's ICT has developed in the past 30 years of economic reform, this book will address the appropriateness and effectiveness of China's ICT strategy, the development trend and the opportunities and challenges that China is facing in the twenty-first century, which will have significant implications for government decision makers and both public and private sectors, as well as Sino-foreign enterprises.

Though facing considerable challenges in its quest to become a world innovation leader in the ICT sector, China offers significant opportunities both for mutually beneficial cooperation in research and education and for trade of knowledge-intensive goods and services. China's opening to the world, encouragement of technology transfer, promotion of information exchange, prioritization of innovation and desire to acquire knowledge and technology provide important opportunities and vehicles for the international community to establish cooperation on issues of global relevance, including environmental protection and corporate social responsibility. For the international community, China's aspirations to become a global knowledge transfer centre in sectors like ICT or nanotechnology could be a positive development providing opportunities rather than a threat.

## Aims and objectives

Based on fresh information obtained from conversations with senior figures of Chinese and foreign enterprises in the Chinese telecommunications industry, this book presents a unique review and comprehensive analysis of the evolution of the Chinese ICT industry. It especially analyses the strengths, weaknesses, opportunities and threats facing both Chinese enterprise and new Western entrants, and the significant implications of China's accession into the WTO.

The current mechanism and various aspects of modern China's ICT sector have been investigated. Our primary aim is to map out the industrial structure and dynamics in the world's fastest – growing economy. The results may ultimately inform decision makers in the ICT sector both in the West and China.

In particular, the main objectives of the book are:

- To examine the evolutionary process of China's ICT and capture the patterns and drivers in such a process
- To debate appropriate models of ICT collaboration between Western countries and China
- To provide strategic insights for the establishment of academic collaboration programmes at institutional level with examination of what is happening in ICT collaboration
- To discuss the appropriateness and effectiveness of China's hi-tech strategy, in particular the strategy of China's ICT industry
- To identify and predict the development trend of China's highway of ICT.

## Summary

The distinctiveness of this book lies in providing strategic insights into China's highway of ICT and addressing the pressing challenges that both Chinese and foreign ICT enterprises are facing. We found it had been an increasing challenge for not only the developing nations to break through boundaries of imitation, but also for many MNCs in big developing countries like China to increase innovation capability through co-evolution with the indigenous companies.

However, the reality is much more complicated than that and hardly rests on such a simple black-and-white trade-off. Indeed, we now know that the challenge China is facing is multifaceted. Here we will debate a number of important issues, that is, competition and cooperation, internationalization and localization, technology strategy, technology transfer, technological evolution and revolution within the sector. We have conducted an in-depth empirical study on China's telecommunications industry. Interviews were conducted with key managers from the two existing mobile operators and some government regulatory officials. Secondary data was collected from government statistics, industry reports and other corporate reports. The data on the industry development, collected over a period of time, will be used for in-depth analysis. Furthermore, this book will provide some in-depth studies of most successful cases, such as Lenovo, Huawei, Haier, SINA, Alibaba and TCL.

The ICT industry serves as the basic, pioneering, supporting and strategic industry of the national economy and has an increasingly critical role in promoting the domestic economy, national safety, the welfare of citizens and social development in this developing country with more than 1.3 billion people. It will increasingly impact on the rest of the world.

# 2
# Pragmatic Development of the ICT Industry

## Introduction

The emergence of a significant "digital divide" between industrialized and developing countries is reproducing existing patterns of inequality with regard to these new information and communication technologies (Castells, 1996). With the trend of global communication deregulation, numerous telecom monopolies have been broken up, enabling new players to emerge in the growing marketplace. Continuing technological innovations like digitalization in computing and communications sectors have made the internet and associated web services available worldwide. Consequently, the great demand for telecom infrastructure equipment and related software products has skyrocketed, bringing remarkable growth to the ICT industry in the past few years.

The Chinese ICT industry is composed of manufacturers and service sectors. The industry has gone through a long and arduous process to establish its primary competitiveness globally.

During China's autarky policy period of 1949–1978, there was no foreign direct investment (FDI) in China's ICT sectors owing to the closed-door policy. China was not able to absorb advanced information and communications technology from Western countries, and the level of domestic technological capability was very low, being mainly limited to basic electronics equipment maintenance.

At that time, information and communications service was just considered as an instrument for government and military use. The Ministry of Posts and Telecommunications (MPT) adopted a highly centralized form of administrative solution to the information and communications sector. As a result, the telecommunications system was operated and managed on a nationwide basis in a semi-military style (Xu & Pitt, 2002). On the other hand, China Telecom, China's only telecom service provider, had to buy equipment from several incumbent domestic suppliers with out-of-date technologies. This led to a low-efficiency and low-quality telecom network with an extremely low user penetration rate, compared with other nations; the telecommunications system and infrastructure in China became one of the poorest in the world before the 1980s.

There were only 3,972,000 telephone lines for a population of over 900 million, with about 4 phones per 1000 people in 1978 (Wu, 2002). The luxury of the residential telephone was only available to senior government officials as a symbol of political status rather than a commercial service based on the principle of universal provision. For ordinary people even in big cities like Shanghai or Beijing, making a long-distance phone call then often involved several hours of effort.

In 1978 China entered an era called the "system reform and market opening". The traditional socialist regime began to undergo a series of reforms towards "socialist market economy". The information infrastructure was considered critical, by the national leaders, to China's modernization ambitions. Those telecommunication service enterprises began to realize that they should not only fulfill the government plan but also meet the demands of the market and sustain their own development. In the turnaround period before 1994, the telecommunications operators, although they were also owned by the state, had the rights to make investment decision under government policy. During this period, the telecommunications demands were vast and increased rapidly (Zhang *et al.*, 2007).

Chinese policy makers led the development of the domestic information technology infrastructure. From 1988 to 1992 the State Economics Committee, the newly formed Ministry of Machine and Electronics, and the State Science Committee focused their joint efforts on developing the broader application of electronics and information technology. And in the early 1990s the State Informatisation Expert Group invested heavily in accelerating the adoption of IT in key sectors of the Chinese economy and infrastructure through large-scale projects such as the Golden Card (adoption of IT in banking system), Golden Bridge (construction of a national telecommunications backbone and other networks) and Golden Customs (computer networking for foreign trading and other related systems).

## China National Information Infrastructure (CNII)

### Objectives of CNII

In 1993, to speed up the progress of the information society, various national information application projects were proposed. Several key projects such as Golden Bridge, Golden Card and Golden Customs were planned to be applied in government, banks, customs and taxation departments and enterprises. These national projects, in addition to building telecommunication backbones, constitute the main platform of CNII (Ure and Liang, 1999). It was hoped the CNII plan would be the main contribution of the information age to China's "Four Modernizations" ambitions in industry, agriculture, science and technology and national defence. Stage one of CNII was up to the year 2000, stage two to the year 2010, and stage three is beyond 2010. The immediate tasks to 2000 included the overall plan for the CNII, development of public information through databases, integration and standardization of data traffic systems, access to the CNII, move towards digital broadcasting, development of regional information systems, electronic informatization building as a "pillar" industry, development of education about informatization, and establishment of efficient administrative and management systems. The guidelines announced for the CNII were centralized planning and direction, unified standards and coordination of building networks to avoid waste of resources. The principles were also enunciated as follows:

- CNII development would be market driven, under government control and regulation.
- The functions of government and enterprise management would be clearly separated.
- Chinese sovereignty and security would be protected.
- Military, civilian and public and non-public networks would be coordinated.
- Technological research, development and technology transfer would be promoted.
- The development focus would be on practical applications which fitted local circumstances.

- A framework of laws and regulations was required to ensure proper control and management of the CNII.

There were 112 national computer information systems based on the public network. A systematic framework was set up and carried out functions of information collecting, processing, storing and application. From the end of the 1990s, as an integral part of China's technology strategy, the projects of e-government and e-business were pushed ahead, effectively strengthening infrastructure construction (Yuan *et al.*, 2004).

### The progress of CNII

In July 1994, limited competition in the wireless sector was finally introduced with the entry of China Unicom, which launched the advanced digital mobile service to challenge the analogue network operation of China Telecom. In 1994, the former MPT formally announced that the telecommunications infrastructure in China was finally able to satisfy the basic demand of the public and the economy. This was a critical turning point – the Chinese telecommunications market began to turn from a sellers' market into a buyers' market (Kan, 1999). State-budgeted expenditure as a percentage of total investment in telecommunications fell from 90% in 1978 to 39% in 1982 to 2% in 1993 (China Statistical Yearbook, various years).

### Internet and broadband service

The internet is seen as the real starting point for the e-infrastructure in China. China's internet began with a few academic networks in late 1980s, with substantial growth occurring from 1994 (Mueller and Tan, 1997). At that time, only a small proportion of the population was connected to the internet and these users were mainly government employees and professional researchers. Promoting the penetration of the internet is consistent with China's development strategy and industrial policy. The number of computer hosts has increased dramatically especially since the year 2000. However, China's internet population has seen a remarkable increase over the past few years in absolute terms (see Table 2.1).

By the end of 2002, the number of internet users in China had increased from 25.4 million to 59.1 million, an annual growth of 75%. China has overtaken Japan to become the world's next largest population of internet users, second only to the US, although its size relative to its 1.3 billion people is still quite low (CNNIC, 2003). China has also become the largest market for mobile communications in the world after 14 years of government-led development without privatization.

According to the Tenth Five-Year Plan (2001–2005) of Information Industry, approved by the State Council, China was to become a modern information society with a large scale and technologically advanced national information infrastructure by 2010. The information and telecommunications industry will be the most important industry in the national economy. It appears that emerging technologies like 3G or Beyond 3G mobile systems, IPTV (Internet Protocol Television) and wireless video-stream will play a key role at that time.

From this perspective, the future of e-government and e-business development in China is promising, although there are still some serious financial obstacles like online payment. Most of the e-infrastructure in China is still concentrated in the major coastal cities, and central government encourages the operators to improve the networks in western and outlying regions. Table 2.1 shows the rapid increase in internet and broadband users in China.

*Table 2.1* Growth of internet and broadband service in China

|  | 1998 | 2000 | 2002 | 2004 | 2006 |
|---|---|---|---|---|---|
| Number of internet users (millions) | 2.1 | 8.9 | 59.1 | 94.0 | 137.0 |
| Number of broadband users (millions) | / | / | 6.6 | 42.8 | 90.7 |

*Source*: China Internet Network Information Center (CNNIC).

## The rise of the telecommunication service industry

In fact, China's telecommunications sector has also been growing faster than the economy as a whole, expanding at an annual rate of 30–50% since 1989 (Tan, 1997). Taking the investment of telecommunications network as an example, around 80% of investment in the telecommunications infrastructure has come directly from revenue sources, of which 35% has come from installation or connection charges and 40% from usage charges (Ure and Liang, 1999).

Also, in May 1999, the MII announced that it would invest up to ¥1 billion ($120 million) for domestic manufacturers to manufacture cellular handsets, funded by a 5% tax on handset sales. The stated goal was to help domestic handset brands reach 50% market share in three years. When the incentives prompted thirty Chinese companies to enter the market, in November 1999 the government chose nine firms as authorized manufacturers, with TV makers Konka and TCL joining established telecom producers such as Huawei Technologies, Zhongxing Telecom (ZTE) and Eastern Communications (Eastcomm).

In July 2001, the Ministry of Information Industry (MII) of the People's Republic of China announced that the number of its mobile phone users had reached 120.6 million, which made China the largest mobile communication user market in the world after 14 years of government-led development without privatization (Ure and Liang, 1999). The industry had achieved sustained development despite the sluggish development of the global telecommunications market. The number of mobile subscribers in China doubled each year from 1994 to 2001. By the end of 2006 China had 461.1 million mobile telecommunication subscribers (MII, 2006) and had become one of the hottest spots for the international and domestic telecom operators, equipment and phone manufacturers.

At the end of 2003, there were six facilities-based telecom operators at the national level who had deployed telecom lines and facilities and provided services. Table 2.2 shows the exponential growth of the telephone penetration rate in China since 1998. The main fixed lines in operation reached 367.8 million. The number of its mobile phone users reached 461.1 million at the end of 2006 with a penetration of 35.3%.

*Table 2.2*  Growth of telecommunication service in China

|  | 1998 | 2000 | 2002 | 2004 | 2006 |
|---|---|---|---|---|---|
| Main fixed lines in operation (thousands) | 87,420 | 144,829 | 214,419 | 312,443 | 367,812 |
| Main fixed lines per 100 inhabitants | 7 | 11.3 | 16.8 | 23.9 | 28.1 |
| Mobile telephone subscribers (thousands) | 23,863 | 85,260 | 206,270 | 334,824 | 461,082 |
| Mobile subscribers per 100 inhabitants | 1.9 | 6.67 | 16.19 | 25.6 | 35.3 |

*Source*: MII.

## Ever-changing service industry structure

The most revolutionary step and development strategy taken by the MII since its establishment was to split the former China Telecom into four independent groups in mid-1999, namely China Telecom, China Mobile, China Satellite and GuoXin Paging Company. The regulator adopted a strategy of "vertical separation" and the former China Telecom was finally split up into these four groups according to specific services. New China Telecom, however, only retained responsibility for fixed network services and China Mobile is specifically dedicated to mobile phone services; China Satellite is specific to satellite communications, while GuoXin Paging Company focuses on radio paging services only. These new operators are financially and operationally independent. The GuoXin Paging Company was subsequently merged with China Unicom as a measure to enhance China Unicom's financial strengths.

In May 2002, China Telecom was reorganized nationwide. It retained only 70% of its backbone network in South China. The other 30% of the network was handed over to the new China Netcom Group, formed by the merging of China Netcom and Jitong. This policy offered the full range of fixed telecommunications, mobile phone, data connection, and other basic telecommunications services, and substantially promoted the degree of competition within China's telecommunications industry.

Building telecom infrastructure requires huge amounts of capital. However, it takes time to sign up fee-paying subscribers and to build revenue streams from telecom services. Obtaining the necessary capital for network deployment is a critical issue, particularly for new telecom service giants, so it was natural that they would seek financial assistance from international capital markets. After successfully going public in the Hong Kong and New York stock exchanges, the four biggest Chinese Telecommunication Operators must follow the principles of capital markets. In May 2008, the reform is designed to foster "healthy market competition and prevent a monopoly by any", according to a joint statement, issued by the Ministry of Industry and Information, Ministry of Finance, and the National Development and Reform Commission. The structural overhaul was expected to have a long-lasting effect on a massive and rapidly growing market (Chinadaily, 2008).

China Mobile Communications, the state-owned parent of China Mobile, which is listed in Hong Kong, will take control of fixed-line operator China Tietong Telecommunications Corporation. Tietong, which means "railway telecom" in Chinese, had assets of 55.3 billion RMB. China Mobile, with more than two-thirds of the nation's mobilephone users as of 30 April 2008, posted a profit of 87.1 billion RMB in 2007. The company's domination of China's wireless market has helped its stock triple in the past two years, overtaking General Electric and Microsoft to become the world's fourth largest company by market value.

China Telecom, China's biggest fixed-line company, will acquire Unicom's smaller mobile phone network, which provides services to 43 million customers based on the code-division multiple access technology used in Japan and South Korea. China Telecom will also get China Satellite Communications Corporation's phone assets. China Network Communications Corporation will merge with Unicom's parent to offer fixed-line and mobile phone services based on the global system for mobile communications technology that is used in most of the world. Unicom had 125.4 million Global System for Mobile communication (GSM) customers as of the end of April 2008, according to the company. Netcom, the nation's second largest fixed-line company, had 108 million phone users. Chinese regulators aim to boost competition between fixed-line operators before the nation rolls out 3G high-speed wireless services, which will require billions of dollars in investment for network equipment.

Several policy instruments are adopted to adjust the changing status of the industry structure. These policy instruments include price regulation such as installation fees and call costs per minute; standard setting such as the introduction decision on GSM and Code Division Multiple Access (CDMA) systems; direct administration such as appointing top officials of the operators. As to the potential entrants, the government will decide on the number and the timing of new license issue.

The firm's behaviour and the performance of the marketplace can also be observed in the framework. Under the supervision of the government, we can see that the two state-owned mobile operators tried to react to the fierce competition quickly and proactively. They penetrated the market with flexible tariffs, new services and upgraded networks. And the purchasing desires of the potential customers were triggered by the improved services, customized contents and flexible prices.

The policy design of the competitive market has really stimulated the recent quick growth of the mobile telecommunications industry in China. However, there remain some unsolved problems which need special attention. For historical reasons, MII has a deep-rooted and intimate relationship with China Mobile, China Unicom, and other regulated operators. China's mobile telecommunication service industry is still administration-based. The frequent policy interventions by the government inevitably mean that there are still many uncertainties about the future industry development of this fastest emerging economy.

## Dealing with the digital divide

China is a vast country and the penetration rate of ICT services is very uneven across the regions. There has always been great regional variation in China's economic development. The standard of living is relatively high in the southern provinces and coastal areas. In fact, people in these areas have benefited the most from China's economic growth and ICT infrastructure. The country's 31 provinces, autonomous regions and cities under direct guidance of the central government are geographically categorized into three zones: the eastern, the central and the western zones. In terms of economic development, the eastern region is the most advanced, followed by the central region and finally by the backward western region.

One strategy for providing universal communication service involves first narrowing regional gaps in penetration levels. The close relation between expansion of the telecom industry and economic development suggests that regional targeting can make economic sense. Clearly, given its unique circumstances, China should follow its own path in formulating a regulatory regime for universal service as there seems to be no one model currently in use elsewhere in the world which can be readily transplanted wholesale into China's institutional environment.

China commenced launching the Village Access Project (VAP) in 2004 as an interim institutional arrangement in which access tasks are distributed among the six incumbent carriers to address the pressing issue of providing basic telephone services to its rural areas. By the end of 2007, China's government had managed to connect roughly 99.5% of its total administrative villages, each with at least two workable telephone lines (MII, 2008). In doing so, the six national carriers have committed RMB 540 million to extending networks to rural areas by the end of 2006 (MII, 2007).

The central government is currently launching an even more ambitious goal of further promoting telephone penetration as well as internet diffusion in its vast rural areas (Committee, 2005). The objective of this drive can be briefly summarized as extending "telephony to every village and broadband to every township" by the end of the eleventh Five Year Plan. Political and ideological forces are now inclined to go even further to advocate a new round of large-scale crusades to eventually deploy most ICT services to every corner of rural China (MII, 2006).

## The equipment manufacturing sectors

At the beginning of the 1980s, China was still heavily dependent on foreign manufacturing companies for telecommunications equipment and technology. Its close proximity to the growing Asia Pacific market also reinforced China's status as an ideal manufacturing location, especially for those global telecom manufacturers. Echoing the market growth, most of the global leading firms started their operations in China in the 1980s and 1990s: Cisco, Ericsson, Lucent Technologies, Motorola, Nokia, Nortel Networks and Siemens. Among the seven MNCs, Siemens and Motorola have the most employees (20,000 and 13,000 respectively). And Motorola distinguishes itself by its large investment in China. By 2002, it had invested $3.4 billion since it first established subsidiaries in China back in 1987.

Since the late 1980s, some emerging local manufacturing firms have arisen. Huawei and ZTE were established in the middle of the 1980s, while DTT and GDT were established in the middle of the 1990s. At the beginning, China's telecommunications equipment market has been largely production driven, whereby value is created from basic production, mainly of low-end routers and switch products. Since the late 1990s some domestic firms like Huawei and ZTE have begun to emerge as serious competitors to the MNCs in the domestic market. These leading indigenous firms, which aim to catch up with rivals in developed countries, have recently been trying to emerge as serious high-tech competitors not only in domestic markets but also global markets.

Security and image concerns have shaped China's thinking about the core competences in the high-tech sector and have often been connected with dissatisfaction with domination by foreign multi-nationals. Government has also put vast investment into core trans-mission technologies like Dense Wavelength Division Multiplexing (DWDM) backbones. China Netcom, one of the new telecommunica-tions operators, was specially established for the commercial trial for DWDM backbone with 40GB per second broadband in 1999. China's market size and increasingly capable technical community give it unique advantages in challenging the established global technological architecture.

Then there were breakthroughs in key technologies such as program controlled switchboards, digital mobile telecommunication, DWDM, Synchronous Digital Hierarchy (SDH) and Asynchronous Transfer Mode (ATM), etc., which have enabled China to become one of the countries owning advanced technologies in the world within a short period of time.

Digital technologies were widely applied in the audio-visual area. New products came out one after another. China successfully devel-oped HDTV sample systems. Domestic produced microcomputers have reached international standards. New products were launched at the same time as in the international market. There were techno-logical breakthroughs in producing high performance computers and high-speed routers.

The key driving forces have brought about a transformation from production-orientation to technology-orientation and finally to indigenous innovation-orientation. During this period, China was transforming from attracting large multinational investors to encour-aging the local indigenous companies. In this sector, the emphasis on collaboration with MNCs has also transformed unidirectional tech-nology licensing into co-development. After entry into the WTO, China hopes to catch the opportunity of emerging digital commu-nications technology by developing TD-SCDMA, its own 3G system, to stimulate its sustainable socio-economic development.

In July 1997, the Chinese government established a 3G technology assessment group in Beijing which began to visualize the future of the next generation ICT technology in China. At that time, China was considering three rival technologies as the standard for future 3G networks. These were Qualcomm's CDMA2000, which builds on the code division multiple access, used as standard by China Unicom; Wideband CDMA, which is backed by European companies and builds on the GSM, used as standard by China Mobile; and Time Division-Synchronous CDMA, or TD-SCDMA, a homegrown technology developed by China's Datang Mobile Communications Equipment Co. and Germany's Siemens AG. TD-SCDMA, one of the 3G standards sponsored by China, has the potential to produce significant added value in the future, and it has achieved financial support from central government. With a population of 1.3 billion, the choice of 3G system standards by China seems to have a remarkable impact on the future of the mobile telecommunications industry worldwide.

Figure 2.1 shows the stages of development in China's ICT equipment industry since the 1980s. The underlying institutional environment has changed from an open market through WTO entry to the development of China's own standards, and the key driving forces have changed from production through technology then to indigenous innovation, while collaboration with MNCs has changed from uni-directional technology licensing to co-development between the domestic and foreign firms.

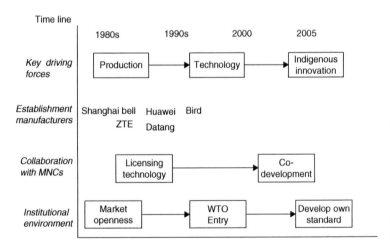

*Figure 2.1* Stages of development in China's ICT equipment industry since the 1980s

After a value decline in 2002, the Chinese communications equipment market has recovered to post steady rates of growth. It is currently the most lucrative market in the Asia-Pacific region. The Chinese communications equipment market generated total revenues of \$25.1 billion in 2005, this representing a compound annual growth rate (CAGR) of 2.7% for the five-year period spanning 2001–2005. In 2005, China accounted for 27.3% of the Asia-Pacific communications equipment market's value. In comparison, Japan generated a further 25.9% of the regional market's revenues (Data monitor, 2006).

The Chinese government insists that its intervention in setting technological standards for the operators makes it possible to realize network externalities faster and reduce the technological or economic uncertainty. By intervening in the operators' standard setting, the Chinese government will continue to have a great influence on the technical direction of existing or potential mobile operators. Unlike the 3G auction practices in European countries, 3G licenses in China will be granted to the state-owned operators through an administrative tender procedure. The commercialization progress of the home-grown TD-SCDMA standard will be an important factor in the decision-making process of the regulator.

It seems that the more political, social, and community dynamics will affect China to make the trade-offs among three alternative 3G systems choices. On the other hand, since the Chinese telecommunications market is as disparate as the nation's economic development, the 2G and 3G mobile networks will co-exist for a long time in China.

The interactions among the actors – policy interventions and market competition – are found to be the key drivers that form the evolution pattern of the industry and push it forward. The regulatory environment in China has greatly shaped the telecommunications industry structure, influenced the behavior of firms and the performance of the industry. Both the telecommunications sector and the general public have benefited from the introduction of effective competition between the two mobile players instead of a monopoly by the incumbent alone. There are still many uncertainties about future development owing to the frequent policy interventions. Furthermore, the industry will try to resolve the trade-offs between alternative technical choices of 3G mobile systems from the political, social and community perspectives. Undoubtedly China, with its great potential market, hopes to play a more proactive and significant role in future in the 3G area.

## Building the domestic handset industry

Attracted by the high profits and low competition in the Chinese mobile phone industry, at the end of the 1990s many Chinese domestic firms were drawn into producing GSM mobile phones. The number of mobile phone manufacturers in China grew from five firms in 1997 to thirty-seven in 2005. Most Chinese cellphone manufacturers pursue an outsourcing strategy instead of conducting research and development (R&D) in-house. We also found that total shipments and the proportion of surface mount technology (SMT) remain low. Since local vendors depend on outsourcing, the ratio of local manufacturers' SMT self-assembled shipments to total local manufacturers' shipments has declined significantly. Similarly, because local vendors are heavily dependent on outsourcing, the ratio of local manufacturers' own technology shipments to total local manufacturers' shipments has not decreased significantly.

Domestic handset manufacturing vendors, such as TCL, Ningbo Bird and Konka, cooperated with South Korean and Taiwanese Original design manufacturers (ODMs) to create and design new handset models. After China joined the WTO in December 2001, its cell phone industry policy focused on expanding the market share of domestic brands. After 2002, foreign handset makers experienced a decline in market share. By limiting the proportion of imports/exports and number of licenses, and by controlling the purchase of domestic components, domestic cell phone vendors have taken over 50% of China's cell phone market. China's potential mobile market has nurtured the domestic handset industry, though it is still very weak.

The Chinese government encouraged domestic companies to capture market share from well-known brands, but the companies usually adopted outsourcing strategies that included allowing foreign companies to design and manufacture their products. The government's industrial policy in this communication sector was a major help in capturing market share but did not encourage the R&D capability of domestic vendors. Viable brand manufacturers with high technological capability have not in fact emerged.

## The survival of the software industry

Although China's hardware manufacturing industry is better known in the world, software has become an official part of the strategy for new industrial development. China's tenth Five-Year Plan (2001–2005) identified software as a critical or "pillar" industry that is essential to economic progress and national security and hence deserving of government promotion. This targeting reflects the recognition that software remains a small and underdeveloped sector. It is an extremely fragmented industry that consists of thousands of small, underdeveloped firms with few competitive advantages relative to the foreign corporations that dominate the market. At the same time, Chinese software output has grown by an average annual rate of 30% since 1995 and is predicted to continue this rapid growth for several more years.

And the industry appears a threat to more established producers like Japan and India because it is located in the world's fastest growing market alongside a dynamic IT manufacturing sector. In the early 1980s, the original issue of local software and hardware was intertwined, since many firms developed technologies that involved some amount of software, often embedded in hardware. A couple of Chinese computer firms, including Founder and Legend, developed the complementary software products. This allowed Founder to establish its early market dominance in Chinese language publishing systems. Chinese programmers at the Institute of Software at the Chinese Academy of Sciences and other research institutes also began to develop simple information systems, typically by directly manipulating a database for a limited set of functions such as searching and reporting, or the ability to update information interactively. These systems were developed separately for particular end users and little attention was given to integration or overall design.

However, the domestic industry is very fragmented, with thousands of very small enterprises with fewer than 50 employees that lack economies of scale or distinctive competencies. These firms typically focus on developing niche applications tailored to particular needs in the domestic market (e.g. systems integration or specialized financial software developed for China's unique accounting practices) and adopting products to Chinese language platforms (e.g. education software). For example, UFSoft and Kingdee are the only domestic software companies ranked in the top ten. This reflects their dominance in the financial software market – the two firms account for about 60% of China's accounting software market – and increasingly the market for enterprise eesource management software. This is due primarily to their privileged knowledge of Chinese financial and managerial practices. They have also benefited from the preferential purchasing practices of Chinese government agencies.

Only a handful of domestic companies have gained control of particular products and acquired global customers. In all of these, the government has had a profound influence in its provision of intellectual capital, training and financial incentives. Some examples of the projects include various large-scale government-funded projects dedicated to developing Chinese competence in core computer technologies, such as the Ministry of Science and Technology's 863 research programme and other government research projects that became the basis for Founder, Legend and other companies. A series of 'golden' government projects were started to expand the country's e-commerce infrastructure and various sectoral applications, such as different e-government programs (Lovelock *et al.*, 1997). Furthermore, almost all the security software firms had a basis in university or government research.

This PC market was so large that it could comfortably sustain the expansion of a number of domestic manufacturers. The market has also stimulated the growth of local software industry but not at the rate some experts expected. Since 2007, the strategy of "industrialization driven by informatization and informatization promoted by industrialization" has been changed to "uniting industrialization and informatization" and industrial software represents another group of customers. In this case, industrial customers manufacture and sell products using third party software, which is supplied by the software companies. Systems software like operating systems and middleware requires fairly advanced or new technology. China has had a few companies that were successful at developing their own operating systems. Again, because these one-off projects are effectively services for specialized software, Chinese firms have an advantage, since multinationals are not in the game of providing such services. It is simply too labour intensive and the lack of increasing returns makes it only worthwhile to specialized service firms (Tschang & Xue, 2003).

The software industry remains the weakest link in China's ICT sectors. In 1995 software products accounted for only 10% of total Chinese IT output, or 68 million RMB ($8.2 million) and the proportion had barely increased by 2000. Software services outpaced the growth of products somewhat, and reached $42.2 billion in 2005. The development of a dynamic software industry, unlike computer or even semiconductor manufacturing, requires more than the ability to mobilize resources quickly; it requires soft and intangible skills that are scarce in China such as creativity, technical experience and managerial know-how as well as the capacity for commercialization (Saxenian, 2003).

This would argue for the development of management and technical capabilities in the Chinese software industry, while allowing India to focus on higher value-added activities. China's leading telecommunications equipment vendor, Huawei, already has a software centre in Bangalore that employs some 400 Indian programmers. However Indian companies possess what Chinese software firms will continue to lack for a long time to come: excellent English language skills; the ability to conduct business with Western clients in their cultural idiom; an established channel of clients; and an internationally acclaimed reputation for trustworthiness, reliability and credibility as a provider of skilled services. Moreover, the existence of a big domestic market means that China will never simply follow India's software offshore development strategy; however it is a trend which could help China move away from the total concentration on domestic markets which is currently the case.

Software education with the industry's backing has attracted more attention. In 2001 the State Department of Education authorized the launch of 35 model university-based Software Institutes, with financing from China's banks and from domestic as well as foreign companies. Recognizing the limitations of an education system where memorizing is the predominant method of learning, these institutes are using international textbooks and a corporate management model.

Beijing is the largest software producing district, with a balanced industry structure. Beijing's leading position is in part due to its being a centre for government and leading educational and research institutions, as well as the base for a number of well-known computer firms like Lenovo. The software area in Beijing is mainly located in the

Zhongguancuan area of Haidian district, which has two of the leading universities, Peking and Tsinghua, as well the headquarters and
facilities of a number of important early IT companies. The first six
software institutes in Beijing are associated with elite universities such
as Peking University, Beijing University of Aeronautics and Astronau-
tics and Tsinghua University. Shanghai has fewer companies, but is a
leading centre for overseas investment, finance, and high-tech industries, including electronics and semiconductors. The infrastructure,
universities and local government support are also very strong. However, Shanghai is still not known for any sizeable software companies
other than systems integrators (Tschang & Xue, 2003).

The Chinese software model is quite different from India's in its
pursuit of a domestic-led growth strategy. The links with China's
domestic market and industry were clearly an advantage, although
competition was extremely keen, to the point where, as standards,
technologies and markets mature, there is likely to be a large shakeout
of firms in the coming years. It is in working with domestic manufacturers and end users that Chinese software firms are perhaps the most
successful. It is also the area in which their success is best known.
This is because of the clearer path to making packaged products, and
the branding that is associated with it. The main kinds of knowledge include knowledge of consumer preferences and manufacturers'
needs, and the ability to translate them into products, and where
necessary, R&D.

In accordance with the WTO Information Technology Agreement
China phased out software tariffs by the end of 2003. Foreign suppliers are allowed to provide software support services and have more
freedom in establishing service centres. This should increase the competitiveness of foreign software vendors in China. However software
sold in China must also meet the standards set by the Chinese Platform Standard Committee, which approves the sale of software in
the domestic market. Foreign companies often need to modify their
software products in order to meet these local requirements.

Piracy is still a major concern for foreign investors in China's
software industry. The protection of intellectual property rights has
achieved several milestones since 1991, starting with the implementation of the Copyright Law, followed by China's joining the world community in upholding the Berne Convention and the World Copyright
Convention. China has also agreed to abide by WTO's Agreement on

Trade-Related Aspects of Intellectual Property Rights to achieve better enforcement of IPR protection. In May 1999, the State Council issued a notice to all government organizations urging them to use only licensed software. Recent reports suggest that the central government plans to begin a nationwide inspection program to enhance awareness of protecting copyrighted software in government.

## The semiconductor industry

Since its inception in the 1950s, the semiconductor has become one of the most important industries in the twenty-first century. Among the sub-industries of the whole semiconductor industry, the integrated circuit (IC) design sector holds a key position as the link between the semiconductor chip and the system. It is particularly crucial as technology development moves toward integration of 3C (computer, consumer, and communication) products and SOC (system on a chip) design.

Domestic demand for semiconductors, especially ICs, is growing rapidly in China, stimulated by the development of information technology and advanced telecommunication infrastructures throughout the country, and by growing demand for common consumer products. In fact, the semiconductor manufacturing sector may be the weak link of China's electronics industry; 95% of the electronic products produced in China are in one way or another dependent on semiconductor components imported from the US and Japan.

Technologically speaking, China lacks a deep-rooted scientific foundation in the research of semiconductor technology. It does not have research achievements in physics and electronic technologies as do the United States, nor does it have enormous capacity in material science and foundry equipment as does Japan, which has invested heavily since the 1970s.

In the ninth five-year period (1996–2000), China's semiconductor technology entered a new stage of development. The successful completion of the "909" project shortened the distance between China and the world in IC technology. The China-based Semiconductor Manufacturing International Corporation (SMIC), the flagship of China's semiconductor manufacturing firms, was founded in 2000. With headquarters in Shanghai, SMIC has three 200 mm wafer fabs in its Shanghai mega-fab, two 300 mm wafer fabs in its Beijing mega-fab, a 200 mm wafer fab in Tianjin, and an assembly and testing facility in Chengdu. SMIC also has customer service and marketing offices in the US, Europe and Japan, and a representative office in Hong Kong. SMIC has continued to upgrade and expand through a series of technology agreements with customers that include Texas Instruments, Toshiba, Infineon, Elpida, and Fujitsu. Its fourth fabrication was a 300 mm facility, China's first, located in Beijing, that began production in 2004. Since then, SMIC has entered into agreements with municipal governments elsewhere in China (Wuhan, Chengdu, and Shenzhen) to build and manage additional fabs.

Since 2001, local foundries have been able to support almost 100% of the production capacity that IC designers require and all the packaging and testing work can be completed locally. This has stimulated the quick development of the IC designing sector.

Compared with the fabrication sector, the chip design sector in China is still at an early stage. Its relatively young chip design engineers will need more time to steadily build their experience. The founding conditions of the firms will influence other important outcomes such as the survival and profitability of young firms. Some IC design companies, particularly those whose founders include expatriates returning with foreign experience, are likely to begin to impact global markets in the coming decade. It is too early to predict the eventual relative importance of domestically owned and foreign-owned chip design activity, and whether domestic firms will be involved mostly with contract services or with creating and selling their own chips. The Chinese government has taken many steps in support of chip design firms, some of the largest of whom are state-funded. The support measures include tax reductions, venture investing and bank loans.

There has been major reform in scientific research and development methods and the industrialization of technological innovation has been accelerated. As China has become a significant player in the global IC market, it must extend the scope of international cooperation and speed up its current progress in indigenous technology development. China's IC infrastructure is still immature.

Although the Chinese IC industry is developing very fast, it is far from strong. Scarce capital resources, a lack of R&D mechanisms and language problems are identified as the most obvious obstacles to prevent China's firms from making progress in markets. In fact, many

Chinese semiconductor firms are still in the stage of imitation only. Gaining lead time and exploiting learning curve advantages are the primary methods of appropriating returns and their close proximity to local customers has enabled them to better service customers through maintaining rapid response times by qualified engineering staff. The extensive national sales support structure has established its credibility with domestic and international brand design teams throughout the electronics supply chain. However, lack of peripheral industries (e.g., equipment manufacturing, assembly, and testing) is a major concern for future sustainable growth.

Some advanced chip design by Chinese companies is being done by the design divisions of some of the local systems firms including Huawei and Hisense and a few leading start-ups headed by U.S. returnees. Initially, domestic small- and medium-sized enterprises (SMEs) receive larger positive spillovers from R&D investment made by multinational firms. They are struggling to survive in fierce competition with these leading giants as IPR protection has slowly been improved. In an isolated paradigm, they may find it difficult to make the transition from adopters of overseas technology to innovators in their own right. The development of semiconductor design capabilities is rather seen in the context of the broader development of industrial resources with strong characteristics of vertical integration, with chip design providing a source of technology and cost competitiveness for subcontracted manufacturing and Chinese brand-names. Chinese semiconductor firms have not yet acquired large numbers of patents, either at home or in the United States. This is an indicator that Chinese companies are yet to become significant innovators in this field.

## Next e-commerce giant?

The internet is playing an important role in helping modernize China while the revenue/profit levels for Chinese internet companies are quite low. The development of e-commerce has been nothing short of explosive in recent years. Many believe that its growth and impact can only increase in the future. There has been enormous growth in the sale of goods by US and European firms over the internet.

E-commerce is in its infancy in China. The statistics show that China had a total of 137 million internet users in 2006 (CNNIC, 2007), which had increased by 26 million or 23.4% in the previous year. The internet is gradually being diffused among the population at different levels. There was a relatively rapid increase in internet users aged below 18 and above 30, as was the case for internet users with a secondary school education background and below. Low-income groups have increasingly started to accept the internet.

World attention has been attracted by the rapid increase in the Chinese internet population, while the 298, million users account for 22.9% (up from 8.5% in the same period in 2005) of the total Chinese population of nearly 1.3 billion in 2008. Although China has a great and rapidly expanding number of internet users, the overall penetration of the internet is still quite low and there is a great deal of room for development (CNNIC, 2009).

To summarize, the numbers of internet users, computer hosts, CN domain names, websites, webpages, international bandwidth and IP addresses have changed to varying degrees, though they have generally continued to grow. Compared to the same period in 2007, the growth rates of internet users and computer hosts has risen again; the growth of CN domain names, websites, webpages and international bandwidth has increased rapidly and the number of IP addresses has also reached certain size of 181.2 million. However, gaps still exist between regions. All these facts indicate that the internet in China is in its youth, yet irrational and unresolved issues still exist. China will continue to improve internet infrastructures, diversify network services and make them applied. A faster and more impressive development of the internet in China is foreseeable.

Obviously, the uncertainty and the ambiguity of factors in e-commerce give the developing countries more discretion in exercising their power over transactions. Compared to Western countries, China's market systems are much less developed. For instance, creditworthiness and trust are big problems, and distribution and delivery systems are inadequate. However, China continues to see the expansion of its e-commerce industry in both B2C (business to consumer) and B2B (business to business) sectors. Early B2C websites were started by entrepreneurs with domestic and foreign venture capital, small firms and large enterprises which were involved in a sudden "gold rush." Since 2001, dramatic developments have been seen in the Chinese e-business industry. The impressive annual growth rates of B2B and B2C transactions in recent years, as well as the positive forecasts, show that China is making fast progress in the sector. By the end of 2005, the total on-line transaction volume had reached $68.3 billion (CCID, 2006). Entrepreneurs have come up with various business innovations that enable e-business to gain early adapters in China, even in the absence of some critical infrastructure components such as a credit card system or an efficient delivery system. One of the forces driving e-commerce in China will be foreign investment, especially from the US, and China's accession to the World Trade Organization will accelerate that process. China has taken the first step to participating in the e-commerce arena and the market potential is undoubtedly great. However, Chinese firms are still far behind their global counterparts in terms of real online sales volume. When sales for consumers and businesses are combined, only 3.4% of Chinese firms' total sales are conducted online. In addition, only 8.8% of Chinese firms' websites support online payment.

## Business to Consumer (B2C)

The B2C sector has seen low transaction volumes in spite of its large number of websites. The online payment system was improved by the major innovation of payment by cell phone tariff in the absence of a credit card system. To take Sohu.com, one of the leading internet companies, as an example, E-commerce revenues are earned from direct sales of consumer products through Sohu's website. The prevalent B2C products include books, health care, cosmetics, videos, CDs and computer equipment. Services such as hotel and airline bookings and digital entertainment can be easier to provide since physical delivery may not be involved. In 2008, the B2C market turnover reached 177.6 billion RMB (CCID, 2009).

## Business to Business (B2B)

B2B market volume reached 2,148 billion RMB, with a 40.2% increasing compared with 2007. B2B still dominates the sector in China, accounting for 89.5% of total e-commerce spending in China (CCID, 2009). Entrepreneurs, with the support of domestic and foreign venture capital have started most of China's B2B websites since 1999. However, uncertainty about the return on investment has gradually drained out domestic and foreign venture capital. Many start-ups have disappeared from the playing ground. Meanwhile, large enterprises and government affiliated organizations have started to dominate the B2B sector by buying out existing websites or creating their own sites. This is mostly because large enterprises and government-affiliated organizations have a large pool of IT experts and close ties with the industry. The main reasons for refusing e-commerce given by small and medium sized businesses are the immature social environments and insufficient techniques.

## The future

The future Chinese firms remain at the early stage of e-commerce. Since 2001, China has been aggressively upgrading its technology infrastructure to enable e-commerce diffusion. However, there are barriers to technology progress in business, legal and cultural areas. These factors in combination lead to a very limited amount of actual B2B and B2C online transactions. This is why most Chinese websites do not offer or support online business although there is a large percentage of web presence among Chinese firms. In some special cases such as wireless SMS services where business, legal and cultural barriers are resolved, technology upgrade allows China to experience diffusion on a par with or even beyond other countries.

The service innovation process will have different impacts and conflicting interests among the different players in the industrial system which can facilitate or impede the innovation diffusion. It is quite difficult to launch the innovation process by market mechanisms alone within such a regulated system; it seems that policy interventions are desirable to encourage diffusion by legitimating and spreading the emerging technology. Once the initial launching barriers have been removed or decreased by policy intervention, it is market factors which have the greatest impact on technology improvement, accompanied by price reduction. Undoubtedly, end consumers in a competitive market will finally harvest the benefits from this innovation process.

## The future model

For China, with a vast civilization, a proud economic and political history, it is really difficult to accept that it may be unable to emulate Britain, the US and Japan in building national champions through proactive industrial policy. It is becoming increasingly necessary for China's large reforming enterprises to benchmark themselves realistically against the global giants (Nolan, 2001). In the meantime, China needs an appropriate and effective technology and innovation strategy.

Chinese firms have many disadvantages to overcome; for example, having a big local market with regional protectionism was a safe bet in the past, but not now. Local markets are being invaded by firms from other regions as China develops a national market rather than having simply several regional markets. And foreign firms can now engage in more than production. They can distribute, market, advertise, localize, and conduct R&D. Overseas, foreign firms have major advantages, including local market knowledge that Chinese firms do not yet have. So, what is it that enables Chinese firms to compete?

Unlike the export-oriented countries in South East Asia, the Chinese home market gives domestic companies the opportunity to move directly into own-brand manufacturing rather than moving progressively from manufacturing others' brands to creating their own (OEM to OBM). The export industry and the domestic market in China are not in fact separate spheres; rather, they interact in complicated and evolving ways (Zhou, 2008). We argue that there is a triple alliance of foreign technology, government support, and excellent implementation on the part of the enterprise(s). Is there a Chinese model? The primary aim of benchmarking Chinese firms' competitiveness is to establish a Chinese model. The creation and sustainability of competitive advantage has never been more of a challenge than it is today. Flexibility and adaptability and the ability of both individuals and organizations to learn from their experience and their competitors are now integral elements of a firm's business strategy. Knowing what competitiveness is, an organization must learn about its internal and external relationships and build both hard and soft capacity. However, such learning must take place faster than competitors' in order to deliver sustainable competitive advantage.

## Summary

The combination of telecommunications deregulation, an exponential increase in internet IP applications, and the popularity of mobile voice and data services has created tremendous growth in the information and communications industry for the past several years in China, the biggest developing country.

China's entry into the WTO has increased the transparency and predictability of the business environment and the legal system, with regard to the protection of intellectual property rights. With globalization, China's ICT industry has gone through a long-term process to establish international competitiveness in several sectors: telecom systems, PCs and some consumer electronics products accompanied with an explosive growth in the information infrastructure. Helped by a large influx of foreign capital and expertise, China has in recent years become a major global producer of information-related equipment, including mobile handsets, notebook computers, motherboards, optical disc drives and DSCs. But although many of these products may be considered high-tech, the processes involved in producing them are not. China will still face more challenges in the trip to a technology powerhouse in the global ICT arena.

# 3
# Institutional and Regulatory Environments in ICT Sectors

## Relative roles and policy framework

According to institution literature, institutions can be defined as systems composed of regulative, normative and cultural-cognitive elements that shape social behaviour and social structure (Scott, 1995). These systems combined provide meaning, order and stability in an institutional environment. Institutions are also generally referred to in terms of formal rules (e.g. constitutions, laws and regulations) and informal constraints (e.g. norms, sanctions and conventions). While both organizations and market are embedded in a broader institutional environment, market is an institutional arrangement which provides organizations with access to resources owned by other organizations. Institutional theories underscore the ability of institutions to influence organizations to conform to practices, policies and structures that are consistent with institutional preferences (Meyer & Rowan, 1977). In the transition economies, market mechanism is also subject to institutional influences; in particular, how resources are developed and mobilized among different organizations can be affected by policies on intellectual property and foreign ownership (Zhou & Li, 2007). Under these circumstances, both institutional and market transitions may in fact interact and produce enhancing as well as conflicting forces, with various behavioral consequences (Barnett & Carroll, 1993).

In the past two decades, many researchers have assessed the impact of institutional forces on emerging economies (Hoskisson *et al.*, 2000). The role of institutions in emerging economies is to reduce environmental uncertainty by facilitating interactions among exchange partners (North, 1990). In most countries, institutional changes that gradually relax state ownership and control and provide the incentives for adaptive learning and intellectual property development will encourage more enterprising activities and stimulate improvements in enterprises (Jefferson & Rawski, 1995; Oliver, 1991). However, the development of market-related institutions can be slow and difficult. Public suspicion of foreign firms and missing institutional features, such as lack of well-defined property rights and inability to manage enforcement, have hampered foreign direct investments (FDI). Both political and market pressures can lead to institutional constraints that will slow down the economic reform process and increase transaction costs for enterprises (Peng, 2003).

In fact the industrial and institutional environment and an organization's strategy moderate the effect of organizational factors, such as the management team and firm resources, on international behaviour and competitive advantage. From a regulatory institutional perspective, the roles of industrial policies and laws in China have changed a lot in the past two decades. More than 500 policy documents have been introduced since the economic reform of the 1980s (see http://www.most.gov.cn/eng/policies/regulations/index.htm).   The primary changes are particularly concerned with reducing the dominant role of the government in practical operations. Instead, its role is to provide an effective platform for industrialization of S&T achievements, to increase the supply of resources, to stimulate market demand and to promote talent mobility and international cooperation.

With respect to the institutional environment, China is still in a lengthy transitional stage from traditional planning economy to market economy. Policymaking in China is rather complex and fragmented (Lampton, 1992; Lieberthal, 1992; Shirk, 1992). There are a large number of enterprises and bureaucracies contending for economic advantage and power within China's ICT sector with different involvement in the development of the industry. As to the formal institutions, China has no national legislation in telecommunications. As a result, the overall regulatory regime lacks a solid legal foundation in this sector.

Complex technological systems like modern telecommunications infrastructure are subject to institutional design and the relevant policymakers may have power to influence demand and promote related technical standards. In the international sphere, communications competition has largely been introduced through liberalization and by introducing new competitors. The devolution approach has been used rarely, except for the AT&T case in the US (Noam & Kramer, 1994; Snow, 1995). The work of Noam and Kramer (1994) provides us with an overview of international communications reform and transformation. Specifically, we will consider the changes in industrial structure including liberalization, devolution and consolidation, and regulation reform. While generally the telecommunications sector has moved towards full liberalization and deregulation, on the global scale there is great variation in how this has been achieved in individual countries. Different countries have adopted varying transitional mechanisms in their telecommunications reform process.

## Western experiences

By the end of the last century, the traditional monopoly structure had undergone significant changes, with the US playing a leading role. In the US, AT&T had been the *de facto* monopoly, not only in services and infrastructure, but also in equipment and research. Since AT&T had never been granted a monopoly franchise by the law, the challenge to AT&T's position in the market had been constant, and the market was opened step by step. On January 1, 1984, AT&T was ordered to divest itself of its local service sector, which was regrouped under seven Regional Bell Operating Companies (RBOCs) known as the Baby Bells. Consequently, the regional monopolies became a substitute for the national monopoly in local services, with a prohibition to provide long-distance services and information services, and involvement in equipment manufacturing. Meanwhile AT&T was allowed to enter information services and other sectors outside the regulated telecommunications market as stipulated by the 1956 Consent Decree (Snow, 1995). Widespread wireless technologies have promoted competition in the internet access market. Internet-based services have become the focus of competition. Now in the agenda of Federal Communications Commission (FCC), the overlap of wire-line telecommunications, wireless telecommunications and cable television (CATV) has become pronounced (Wu *et al.*, 2004).

In the UK, a new Telecommunications Act became law in 1984. It abolished BT's exclusive right to public telecommunications services. Meanwhile Mercury's license was widened to become a long-distance carrier competing with BT. This Act also led to the privatization of BT. In three rounds in 1984, 1991 and 1993 the government sold all its interest in BT to the public, and made BT become a publicly quoted company. The Office of Telecommunications (Oftel) was also formed as a regulatory body (Thatcher, 1999). The new law caused the UK telecommunications market to transform continuously in this evolving environment (Lal & Strachan, 2004).

Impelled by Oftel, the government began to liberalize the value-added service (VAS) market and authorize competition in the sale of all types of customer premises equipment. In 1991, by granting new licenses, the government terminated the duopoly structure in the long-distance market. Mobile operators were also allowed to run fixed services. The limit on the number of licenses was lifted, and other telecommunications carriers were allowed to operate mobile networks (Lal & Strachan, 2004). As a result, the UK became the first country in Europe to introduce competitive analogue mobile phone services, and achieved a huge success in deploying the second generation (2G) networks. Further, in as early as May 1998, the UK government announced that the third generation (3G) licenses would be allocated by auction. The stated overall aim for licensing 3G was to secure, for the benefit of UK consumers and the national economy, the economically advantageous development and sustained provision of 3G services in the UK (Hewitt, 2000). Since telecommunications privatization of the incumbent operator in 1984, BT has generally welcomed the opportunity to strategically position itself as a European, and indeed a global, player in the delivery of a constantly increasing and diverse basket of services. The convergence of technologies required the convergence of regulation. As a result, in December 2003, Ofcom (the Office of Communications) was formed to inherit the responsibilities of other regulatory bodies.

## Transformation in major developing countries

In each country, the shape of telecommunications industry reform has been different; each government has used a specific mix of approaches over time to transform the markets (Gao, 2006). The developed world, as described above, followed a gradual reform strategy, whilst in developing countries, both gradual and radical change were employed.

As we shall see, China's ICT regulation and policy are also subject to the constraints of its institutional structure. In the context of the industry's development, many important events occurred initially after China became a member of WTO in 2001. Institutional changes are now being introduced rapidly and markets are increasingly open for competition.

In China, devolution was adopted as a major measure and applied to the Public Telecom Operator (PTO), which was split first by services and function and later by areas. This was carried out because, without necessary laws such as competition and anti-trust laws, the existence of a strong incumbent might influence the institutional environment and jeopardize regulation enforcement and fair competition. Meanwhile, competition enabled the Chinese government to adopt strong restructuring measures in the telecommunications sector. The evolution of China's ICT industry has undoubtedly been a positive step toward further deregulation of the Chinese communications market and ensures more effective regulation of telecommunications operators for the benefit of the wider community. The regulatory environment in China, through policy intervention, fundamentally shapes the competitive landscape of the industry.

## Regulator structure and main regulators

Widespread deregulation in the telecoms industry resulted in the opening up of local, long-distance, international, cable, and cellular telephone markets in many countries. Accompanying this was the break-up of telecoms monopolies, which enabled different emerging competitive carriers to offer a variety of telecom services and forced incumbent monopolies to upgrade their networks and improve overall service.

### From MPT to MII

In November 1949, following the founding of the People's Republic of China, the Ministry of Posts and Telecommunications (MPT) was formally established and was mainly responsible for formulating development plans and coordinating nationwide telecommunications networks. China's telecommunications industry, like other industries, experienced slow development before the late 1970s. During this period, telecommunication service was just considered an instrument for government and military use. The MPT adopted a highly centralized form of administrative control of the information and communication sectors. As a result, the telecommunications system was operated and managed on a nationwide basis in a semi-military style (Xu & Pitt, 2002). Before 1998, China Telecom was the only national operator and could be seen as a collection of separate, state-owned enterprises that provided service at the national, provincial and local levels.

In line with the state, it was in MPT's interests to take advantage of the market monopoly instead of supporting liberalization. In 1989, in order to protect China's telecommunications industry from reforming foreign influence, MPT, representing the central government, issued Decree number 216, which declared that the telecommunications network was a national infrastructure and therefore had to be under the absolute control of the state to guarantee national security and sovereignty (MPT, 1992). Furthermore, MPT persuaded the State Council to grant preferential arrangements to the telecommunications sector to improve the poor status of China's telecommunications infrastructure. MPT claimed that this was necessary as low network efficiency and high costs went hand in hand at the start of large-scale network construction (MII, 1999). This initiative was supported by the state, which needed to ease the bottleneck in the telecommunications industry in its efforts to build a strong national economy. Consequently, in 1991 the State Council enacted Decree number 56 allowing MPT to charge an installation fee from every subscriber equal to the construction cost of one line. MPT defended the interests of the incumbent operator uncompromisingly by creating barriers for new entrants and cared little about the interests of individual customers in China.

In 1994, the operations arm of MPT was renamed the China Telecommunications Corporation (China Telecom) and China United Telecommunications (China Unicom) was set up to foster domestic competition (Becky & Loo, 2004). Although there was no real competition because China Telecom still controlled the only public fixed telephone network (FIX) in China, the appearance of China Unicom was also a prologue to Chinese telecommunications reforms. In 1997, China Telecom (Hong Kong) raised funds in the Hong Kong stock market, enabling foreign investors to hold shares in Hong Kong's protected market for the first time.

In April 1998, as a practical reform step, China's government reshuffled its telecommunications regulatory institutions by replacing the former regulatory body MPT with the Ministry of Information Industry (MII). The MII was formally established as the result of the merger between two ministries, the former MPT and the former MEI (Ministry of Electronic Industry).

The MII is thus an extremely powerful ministry, and all networks and IT manufacturing industries are now subject to MII's regulation. Its main commitments include development strategy formulation, policymaking and overall regulation of the information industry, including telecommunications, IT product manufacturing and the software sector. Several important changes to the situation with MPT have emerged. A single regulator replaced the regulatory authorities scattered in other government departments, and MII has significantly expanded its regulatory authority from telecommunications to cover the broader information industry. This measure effectively overcame the problems of fragmented regulation and multiple regulators by creating a single regulator, MII.

Secondly, and in contrast to MPT, MII cannot involve itself directly in network operations. Regulatory and operational functions were nominally split for the first time in nearly 50 years. Since MII no longer shares any common interest with an incumbent operator, we can see that the regulator currently enjoys a relatively neutral status. The establishment of the MII is undoubtedly a positive step towards further deregulation of the Chinese telecommunications market and ensures more effective regulation of mobile operators for the benefit of the wider community.

Against this background, in April 2000 a devolution approach was employed to separate the mobile sector of China Telecom into an independent body called China Mobile. As a result of liberalization, China Netcom was formed in August 1999 from the state institutions SARFT and CAS. Moreover, the state allowed the telecommunications networks of national railways to enter the public market and China Railcom was established in December 2000 (*People's Daily*, December 26, 2000). Thus, the market became more competitive as the dominant position of China Telecom was reduced and more operators were included in the market.

In May 2002, in order to deal with the potential competition after entry to the WTO, China Telecom was restructured into two parts by area. The northern part was built from eleven northern provincial networks, China Netcom and Jitong, and it adopted the name of China Netcom. Keeping the name of China Telecom, the southern part retained the networks of nineteen other provinces (*People's Daily*, May 16, 2002).

### Broader government administration

We have seen that competition enabled the Chinese government to adopt strong restructuring measures in its telecommunications sector (MII, 1999).

In contrast, telecommunications regulation rests heavily on government administration and intervention. Important players besides MII are the State Council and the State Planning and Development Commission (SPDC). Regulatory policies must gain support from SPDC and approval from the State Council. Moreover, there are many interest groups with great bargaining power which also exert a significant influence on telecommunications regulation and policy, as was reflected during the establishment of Unicom (Lovelock, 1996).

However, some problems which need special attention remain unsolved in this sector. For historical reasons, the regulator has a deep-rooted and intimate relationship with all regulated operators and some key state-owned manufacturers. China's telecommunications industry is still somewhat administration-based. The regulator not only supervises the whole industry, but also holds the power to appoint, promote, and dismiss key officials of China Mobile and China Unicom, and key personnel decisions of the two operators are inevitably made beyond the level of their own boards. So a coherent regulatory system will take time to take shape and frequent policy interventions by the regulators inevitably mean that many uncertainties as to future industry development continue to exist.

Government plans give no indication that current reforms will lead to a future round of privatizations. The key challenge for the MII in the future is to evolve into a truly independent policymaker and regulator, and to move away from its roots of running the industry in a hands-on manner.

## Policy instruments

Several policy instruments have been adopted to reflect the changing status of the industry's structure. As to the potential entrants into ICT sectors, the government will decide on the number and the timing of new license issuing. The policy design on the competitive market structure has really stimulated the recent quick growth of the mobile telecommunication industry in China. Under the supervision of the government, we can see that the two state-owned mobile operators tried to react to the fierce competition quickly and proactively. They flooded the market and attracted potential customers with flexible tariffs, new services and upgraded networks.

## Policy intervention in IP telephony diffusion

By 1999, the industrial reform had achieved some improvements – three new players (China Unicom, China Netcom and Jitong) had entered the data communication market. China Telecom, however, whose subscribers increased very fast and exceeded 100 million in 1999, still retained the biggest market share in the country. In the PSTN (Public Switching Telephone Network) market, the traditional circuit-switched fixed network, China Telecom had a monopoly for over 50 years, setting high entry barriers to potential entrants. The revenue from its long distance PSTN service was RMB 63.5 billion ($7.7 billion) in 1999 (MII, 1999). This fiercely defended sector was the mainstay of China Telecom's business, which it defended with every effort. Entry barriers to the fixed telecommunications market remained as high as they had been several years before. While MII was under pressure to introduce market mechanisms and lower prices in the sector, new entrants were excluded by the high building costs of a new circuit-switched network. Unlike China Telecom, its competitors were keenly interested in new profitable market niches such as long distance voice services.

In 1999, it was difficult for policy makers to find an ideal solution. Even if they did, the capacity to implement the policy would be very much restricted. In countries where Public Telecom Operators (PTOs) are regulated by independent authorities, like Canada, Britain, and the U.S., there is generally less precedent for regulatory agencies to be directly involved in implementation of new technological matters at an operational level (Milne, 1997). The diffusion of innovation in a dynamic system like the telecommunications industry may lead to greatly unequal distribution of benefits.

IP (Internet Protocol) telephony is the term used to describe the technology of carrying voice or fax over IP-based networks such as the internet. Although there were some early applications of internet telephony in 1996 and 1997, it was not until 1998 that services based on this new technology became significant (Wright, 2001; Rinde, 1999). The voice service over IP technology enables businesses and consumers to make phone calls at much lower costs than the traditional PSTN technology. Two key factors have contributed to the cost-effective implementation of IP telephony. Firstly the price of IP equipment like network routers came down quickly. The second key factor has been the reduction in bandwidth cost on international circuits in recent years (Rinde, 1999). The voice quality of IP telephony has been improved with special QoS (Quality of Service) means and generic increasing bandwidth. With the quality upgrade, the users of IP telephony could make a call irrespective of what kind of hardware or software was at either end or in the middle. In China, the potential fixed operator can establish network gateways between its IP backbone and local telephone networks to provide long distance voice services. Through the use of gateways, IP telephony users can connect directly with any other telephone in the world via the IP-based network.

With the rapid penetration of the internet in China, IP telephony service became available in 1999. At that time, emerging IP telephony technology was presented to the whole industrial system, providing an opportunity for reform. Under pressure from the public to break up the monopoly, neither the regulator nor the newcomers in China had any feasible solution. Among existing firms, the attitudes of China Telecom towards innovation were opposite to its competitors'. China Telecom was strongly against innovation for fear of threat to its former business based on traditional circuit switching. On the other hand, the combined backbone bandwidth of China Unicom, China Netcom and Jitong reached 500 million bits persecond in July 2000 (CINIC, 2000) and the new competitors were eager to benefit from the innovation by making use of redundant backbone capacity to support IP Telephony services. Meanwhile, the emerging innovation also gave policymakers a good opportunity to anticipate how the consequences of commercial adoption of IP telephony could greatly alter the existing structure of the industrial system.

The MII decided to open the commercial IP service to activate the fixed telecommunications market. The IP telephony service was defined as a new telecom service and operational licenses were to be granted for it. In April 1999, MII permitted China Telecom, China Unicom and Jitong Corporation to organize field trials of IP telephones for domestic and international long distance IP telephone and fax services. During the trial period, no settlement was made between the newcomers and the incumbent. In May 1999, MII granted an operational license to China Unicom for long-distance IP telephony services in 25 cities, closely followed by Jitong, China Netcom and China Mobile. The Ministry then published several regulations to standardize IP operation, providing technical specifications on the commercial operation of IP telephony. In March 2000, MII announced that the trial was completed and that the result, based on an enthusiastic market response, was positive. Commercial licenses were then formally granted to China Telecom, China Unicom, Jitong and China Netcom for the commercial operation of IP telephony services. Another license was later granted to China Mobile for provision of IP telephony services using wireless application protocol (WAP).

Every new competitor quickly developed an aggressive rollout plan and established network gateways between its backbone networks and the local telephone networks of China Telecom. Their subscribers could make domestic or international long-distance IP phone calls via any dial tone telephone, which meant that every original subscriber of the incumbent could become a potential subscriber of its competitors. The new relationship between regulator and incumbent has given new entrants a favourable bargaining position in network interconnection with China Telecom. With permission from MII, this interconnection was available at any technically feasible point at the request of the new competitors. The new competitors had almost no interconnection fee payable to China Telecom, enabling provision of voice services at only a fraction of current costs. This facilitated the diffusion of IP telephony innovation on the supply side. Though IP telephony services did not meet the requirements of some senior business users (for example, voice quality of early IP telephony), they attracted most potential ordinary customers with their competitive price. IP telephony fees are now set by the respective providers, with IP prices discounted from PSTN prices (set by MII) ranging from 57%, on an average domestic call to 70%, on international calls to the US and Canada, with an IP telephony discount of 63% for other regions of the world. With a completely different cost structure from existing PSTN networks, and a preferential interconnection fee policy for competitors, enabling voice services to be provided at only a fraction of current cost, IP telephony enables the competitors to break the industrial barriers, to penetrate traditional markets and to capture value from the incumbent. The incumbent's attitude to the launch of this emerging innovation is complex. In the long distance voice market, the domination of China Telecom has been greatly challenged by IP telephony service. Facing fierce challenges from other firms, China Telecom finally decided, after several months to embrace the new technology to defend its market position. As a result of innovation diffusion, the fixed telecommunications industry in China ultimately evolved from monopoly to competition.

Some literature forecast that IP telephony would be rapidly adopted in developing countries around 2005 (Rinde, 1999). However, the prediction came true in China much earlier than expected. IP telephony application has grown explosively in the past several years. Launched in 1999, it then accounted for a mere 2% of long distance call minutes. However, this proportion had increased to 4.7% by the end of 2000 and to 32% by the end of 2001 (MII, 2001). Policy intervention by the regulator has stimulated the innovation diffusion process. Under pressure of competition from IP telephony providers, PSTN telephone providers reduced relevant fees in February 2000.

The practice of policy design and intervention by regulators has been discussed in the previous chapters. The policy-promoted diffusion process is here divided into two stages, namely policy formulation and policy implementation. In the first stage, the policymakers' vision of breaking up the monopoly was the trigger for the formulation and launch of policies to promote innovation diffusion. Policy formulation is based on the desirable consequences of adopting further commercialization. Innovation was rapidly diffused after the innovation-based service was legalized. In the second stage, the diffusion process has been facilitated and stimulated by policy implementation.

As a consequence, diffusion finally changed the industry's structure. Through case studies, a brief model of diffusion promoted by policies is developed here to facilitate understanding of the policy mechanism within the diffusion process, showing the interactions between policy-makers and the behaviours of industry players and innovation diffusions. As a result, the monopolistic market structure can be broken up and consumers could finally benefit from the diffusion process. Therefore in some situations, policy intervention could become the trigger launching and facilitating diffusion of emerging innovations in a large developing country such as China.

## SARFT: an important center

SARFT (State Administration of Radio, Film and Television) is an executive branch under the State Council of the People's Republic of China. Its main task is the administration and supervision of the state-owned media and content enterprises engaged in the television, radio, and movie businesses. Figure 3.1 shows the regulatory responsibilities of MII and SARFT.

SARFT directly controls state-owned enterprises at the national level, such as China Central Television and China National Radio, as well as other movie and television studios and other non-business organizations. It is also responsible for censoring any materials that might fail to meet institutional or cultural standards. An example of such activity is the summer 2007 controversy over the television talent show First Heartthrob. In such circumstances, SARFT has banned foreign investment in its radio and cable networks and has forced foreign-funded companies to restructure. Currently, SARFT is preparing to allow foreign and private capital to flow into film production, distribution and exhibition. It is funding technology upgrades to enable China's film industry to survive the country's entry into the World Trade Organization. SARFT is playing a key role in new information technology services like mobile television and wireless music.

Traditionally, central government has always banned SARFT from engaging in telecom operations and the MII from engaging in radio and TV operations, but it has said nothing about broadband capabilities. In fact, the State Council has granted the MII regulatory authority over commercial TV broadcasting companies and has granted SARFT a lot of latitude in regulating the TV industry. Co-ordination between the two main regulators, MII and SARFT will be a key challenge in the future development of the China's ICT industry.

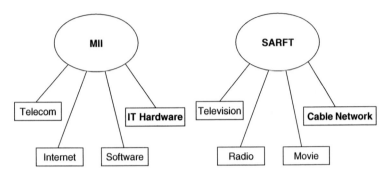

*Figure 3.1*   The regulatory structure of MII and SARFT

While SARFT permits domestic investment in its backbone net-work and value-added services, it does not allow similar practice in its local access networks or basic transmission services. In 1999, the State Council issued Document 82 entitled "Opinions to Strengthen Cable Network Construction and Management" which stipulated that telecom operators could not operate cable TV services and vice versa.

## A case of regulatory conflict: IPTV in China

Recent decades have witnessed dramatic innovation in information technology (IT) towards digital convergence. This new trend of devel-opment brings about new business opportunities (Jelassi and Enders, 2005). New media players have emerged during the process and taken on an increasingly salient role in propelling the process for-ward. This has triggered fierce debate and ambivalence in policy and industrial circles as to whether the new media should be regarded as "commercial industry" or "government undertakings", especially in transitional economies like China.

China's largest telecom operators and broadcast/cable TV providers are now gearing up to deploy products and technologies that will deliver IPTV service in key markets nationwide, creating a potentially huge opportunity for IPTV technology suppliers to tap into one of the world's largest and fastest-growing broadband markets. However, there are many unresolved regulatory issues to be settled before IPTV becomes a major commercial force in China.

Since the late 1990s, voice service using IP technology has enabled businesses and consumers to make phone calls at much lower costs than the traditional PSTN technology. Then the increasing use of broadband networks for transmission of TV and video services has had a radical impact on the characteristics of TV and video services and the deployed business models. IP platforms, due to their inherent interactive component, are changing 'broadcast' in a fundamental way from a broadcast service to an on-demand service.

In 2004, the two incumbent telecommunications operators upgraded and rebuilt their broadband networks and the scale of broadband use has increased quickly. Delivering video over IP presents many new opportunities for the telecommunications operators and equipment vendors. IPTV can help these fixed telecommunications operators to exploit the business potential of broadband networks. As is the case with telecom operators worldwide, China Telecom and China Netcom consider IPTV as a future profitable and desirable service. They are extending their fixed broadband network and services into the realm of video media to enlarge their broadband subscription base and generate revenues from the new value-added services. On the other hand, IPTV development opens up new possibilities for broadcasters in terms of expansion of both numbers and services.

Since 2004, the telecom operating giants have put a big bet on IPTV as one of the top priorities of their business transformations, as IPTV promises a new revenue stream.

In 2004, China Netcom announced that it would change from traditional telecommunications operator to broadband and multimedia service provider. With 6.2 million broadband users, China Netcom strengthened the establishment of the broadband value chain by forming alliances with content providers, internet service providers (ISPs) and equipment manufacturers. The primary focus was on the development of broadband content such as games, education and video, and many popular online games were introduced to stimulate usage and stabilize the revenue per user (China Netcom, 2004).

At the beginning of 2005, China Telecom proposed pushing forward the strategic transformation of the corporation to become a complete information service provider, integrator of internet applications and a leading operator of the integrated information service chain based on the telecom network.

If the established telecommunications operators enter the broadcasting market that offers IPTV services on a large scale, it will be a formidable hit on the traditional cable TV industry of SARFT. To safeguard the challenge of telecommunication sectors, SARFT promulgated decree number thirty-nine, approved by State Council, with the title of Measures for the Administration of the Transmission of Audio-Visual Programmes through the Internet or Other Information Networks. This came into force on October 11, 2004. This helps SARFT regain the control of IPTV services. According to the decree, SARFT will be responsible for the administration of the transmission of audio-visual programmes through the internet and other information networks. The state applies a license system to the transmission of audio-visual programmes through information networks. SARFT will have the authority to issue a license, valid for two years, for transmission of audio-visual programmes through Information Network for those qualified. As to the audio-visual programmes themselves, the decree has extended the administrative authority of SARFT from 'programmes production' to 'programmes transmission', thus greatly strengthening its supervision and administration powers in IPTV. IPTV is thus under heavy regulation in China with respect to licenses for operation as well as content regulation.

The IPTV licenses were only granted to broadcasting firms, and telecommunication companies were forced to cooperate with them to get into the IPTV market. Since the broadcasters, many of which see telecommunications operators as local competitors, were not under any obligation to share IPTV licenses with their potential counterparts, the telecommunications operators were locked out of China's IPTV market if they could not reach an agreement with a licensed broadcasting operator or if the revenue-sharing charge was too high. In May 2005, Shanghai Media Group (SMG) got the first IPTV license and SMG has become a strategically important partner for all the telecom operators as it is currently holder of the only official IPTV license. As to the limited collaboration, the broadcasters dominate the marketing and charging while telecommunication operators only undertake the provision of transmission channels. SARFT also require the licensed broadcaster in collaborative IPTV ventures with telecommunication firms to supervise the content integration platform, manage the broadcasting platform and manage the end-users (Huang & Wang, 2006).

The development of IPTV has met strong resistance from the local broadcasters in some areas. In Fujian Province, Quanzhou Telecom and SMG cooperated on IPTV service. But on December 26, 2005, it was stopped by the local broadcasting regulator. Then on January 10, 2006 the same thing happened in Zhejiang Province and conflict between the telecommunications and broadcasting industries was provoked, thus blocking the market growth of IPTV.

The regulatory challenges related to the IPTV services are a subset of the general convergence process, where the borderline between media, telecom and information technologies vanishes or is at least blurred at the technological level. Obviously, in this development process, a number of different actors are involved that are directly connected to the convergence of the highly regulated media sector and the loosely regulated internet platform. The contradictory regulatory framework structure could not give market players enough certainty to promote relevant investments. The regulatory framework is not used to disclose opportunities to the operators involved but rather to impose limits and reduce possibilities.

## The context of WTO entry

In China's ICT sectors, many important institutional events occurred primarily after China became a member of the WTO on December 11, 2001. Following this, institutional changes are being introduced rapidly and markets are increasingly open for more competition.

The WTO serves as a forum for its members to collectively negotiate to liberalize services which are not covered by the General Agreement on Tariffs and Trade (GATT). In contrast to GATT, one of the most important characteristics of the WTO is that it is a rule-oriented organization. Its multilateral concepts, principles, and rules are legally enforceable and binding on its members (Sauve, 1995, p. 141). The members must take into account the rules-of-law of the WTO while formulating economic policies. Clearly, in the context of the WTO, international law is penetrating the members' domestic formal institutions and playing a much more important role in national policy-making processes than ever before. Legally binding rules of the WTO, as an exogenous formal institution, clearly influence members' domestic institutions including their telecommunications regulation.

However, questions arise when we assess the implementation of WTO rules and principles. For instance, how will domestic institutions react to this newcomer? Will they accommodate it, or resist it, or accept it half-heartedly? Since the rules of the WTO and schedules of commitments presented by the members have to be finally implemented by domestic administrations, the institutional stance in a host country plays a crucial role in determining how far the promised commitments will be implemented. The constraints imposed by institutional endowment in reality produce an institutional equilibrium in which compromises, such as the rules of the WTO, are reached between domestic and international institutions. A regulatory regime's pro-competition institutional stance would actively embrace WTO disciplines, significantly boosting the process of liberalization in the telecommunications sector. But domestic institutions with a counter-regulatory orthodoxy would constitute a significant non-tariff barrier to market entry and effectively frustrate some of the goals of the WTO.

Since there are pervasive and significant differences in political, legislative, judicial and executive systems, among WTO members, as well as resistant and conservative elements, it is unrealistic to believe that implementation of the WTO rules would be homogeneous. There is also a chance for opportunistic members to act as free riders, for example obtaining benefits from other countries fully enforcing their commitments, while effectively circumventing WTO obligations. Typically, differences in institutional stance toward the WTO can account for the significant variation in the scope and depth of the commitments presented by the members, which are exhibited in some empirical studies (Aronson, 1997). Their studies show that countries with pro-competition institutional stances are more likely to make greater commitments than those with the opposite attitudes.

The WTO Fourth Protocol sends a clear signal to countries wishing access to the WTO that they must liberalize telecommunications services and make commitments to regulatory reform. Interestingly, the impact of the WTO on China's telecommunications sector happened even before China assumed formal membership of the WTO.

Although the WTO principles and disciplines do have positive effects in promoting telecommunications liberalization among its members, actual progress towards WTO goals will vary greatly and depend mainly on specific institutional endowments and regulatory stances of the members. From the point of view of the General Agreement on Trade in Services under WTO (WTO/GATS), the best way to implement the WTO Fourth Protocol would be to engage the members' regulators and assist them in realizing a transition toward pro-competition institutions. Specifically, ensuring that the regulatory institutions and stances of the countries which actively incorporate rather than passively resist the WTO disciplines is central to determining the pace and effects of transition. Even with this, it is argued here that the overall domestic institutional endowment and regulatory stance would be finally decisive. Commitments made by the members would make sense only if the implementation of the WTO Fourth Protocol becomes a self-enforcing action driven by the members themselves in the context of a cooperative regulatory stance toward the exogenous institution of the WTO. In China's telecommunications sector, the conservative regulatory stance may persist into the post-WTO era, and if true, this means that the telecommunications market would be open in name but would still exert constraints.

At the end of 2001, China became a member of the WTO. To fulfil the commitment of WTO membership, China agreed to become more open to the information and communications market. It also agreed to allow foreign operators to take up to a 50% share in some telecommunications companies two years from 2001. Fixed-line phone services will open more gradually to foreign competition, with foreign companies allowed a 49% share after six years. In addition, China would eliminate information technology tariffs by 2005, grant trading and distribution rights by 2003, open internet and telecom markets to investment and services, and provide stronger protection of intellectual property.

If the appraisal contained in this chapter is accurate, the implications are profound. For Chinese regulators, it calls for ongoing regulatory restructuring and specifies the existing regulatory barriers impeding its implementation of commitments on market access and regulatory reform. In the WTO/GATS context, it examines the interaction between the members' domestic institutions and the exogenous rules and disciplines emanating from the WTO. It demonstrates that the national institutional environment and regulatory stance matter in the implementation of the WTO Agreements, and offers a case study of China to exemplify these arguments (Zhang, 2001).

## Judicial institutions

In fact, thus far judicial institutions have rarely played a role in telecommunications regulation. There is no overall telecommunication law, nor institutions to enforce the existing regulations in China. Instead of relying on laws, which has generally been the case in other countries, regulation has been conducted mainly by using administrative methods.

An exceptional case occurred at the end of the 1990s. People began privately offering IP telephone services through computer stores in some cities, but soon saw their equipment seized on the basis that their operations were illegal. On January 20, 1999, the Intermediate People's Court in Fuzhou judged that the operation of offering IP telephony service by a private firm is not illegal, a case appealed by the local branch of China Telecom. The judgment stimulated the reconsideration of IP telephony service by the regulatory authority of China. Policy measures have been taken to prevent the incumbent operator from abusing its position to baffle innovation diffusion.

Much attention has been paid by the regulator to a law and ordinance passed in 2000. "The Telecommunications Ordinance of the People's Republic of China" was promulgated by the State Council on September 20, 2000 and came into force on the same day. This regulation become the primary ordinance to cover nearly all aspects of the telecommunications industry, including market admittance, network inter-linkage, charges, resources, service, construction and safety. According to the ordinance, mobile network service belongs to basic telecommunications businesses, any potential entrant is subject to the examination and approval of the MII under the State Council, and must obtain a business license. According to the definition of the ordinance, telecommunication means all the activities of transmitting, sending or receiving sounds, words, data, images or any other kinds of information, through wire-line or wireless electromagnetism or photo-electricity systems. In the meantime, MII is the only department with the jurisdiction to regulate the overall Chinese telecommunications industry.

The government is concerned by the shift to data as this will transfer the problem of information "control" from the internet to the mobile industry. On the other side, and in light of the decreasing Average Revenue Per User (ARPU) in voice communications, operators are welcoming the additional revenue stream. There is thus little doubt that the Chinese operators will cooperate with the government, as do ISPs. In addition to those issues, actors identify additional issues: the emergence of new actors, the partial listing of Chinese operators on foreign capital markets, the current gloom in capital markets, decreasing ARPUs, and the lack of applications.

In most countries the telecommunications market change has been enacted by passing laws. For example, in the UK, the 1984 and 1991 Telecommunications Acts have provided the basis for its market transformation. In the US, the 1996 Telecommunications Act has led to a full liberalization (Thatcher, 1999). In contrast, in China the telecommunications reform has been carried out by simple governmental orders without the supervision of laws. This is the result of adhering to the national policy of reforming the economic system through an "act after trial" process (Gao, 2006).

## Comparison study with India

Most developing countries executed a gradual transformation, India being an example. Here we conduct a comparison study between China and India, two developing countries with the biggest populations. In India, the telecommunications reform progressed by several steps. Until 1985, the Ministry of Posts and Telegraphs controlled the telecommunications services and infrastructure. The sector was mainly governed by the Indian Telegraph Act of 1885. In 1985 postal services were separated from telecommunications (Gupta, 2001). In 1986, limited liberalization began to be introduced in basic telecommunications. Mahanagar Nigam Telephone Limited (MNTL) was established to compete with the state-owned Department of Telecommunications (DoT) in local services in some metropolitan areas. In 1992, competition was allowed in cellular mobile services (Gupta, 2001). In 1994, the Indian government liberalized the market to foreign and private competitors, allowing foreign firms to hold up to 49% of the shares (Petrazzini & Krishnaswamy, 1998). In 1997, in India's commitment to the WTO, it decided to retain a 25%

limitation of share for foreign capitals. This conflicted with the previous policy which set this figure at 49%, as previously mentioned. This controversy ultimately forced the government to pass the Telecom Regulatory Authority of India Act in 1997. Telecom Regulatory Authority of India (TRAI) was formed as the regulatory agency. Moreover, a regional competition structure was adopted in local and mobile services so as to achieve a well-balanced development. In each cellular or wire-line circle, one or two private companies respectively might be licensed. DoT and VSNL were granted a monopoly over intra-circle long distance and international services respectively (Gupta, 2001). In 1998, recognizing the explosive growth of the internet, an internet policy was announced that invited various stakeholders to participate in the consultation process. More than 400 ISPs were awarded licenses, including national, state and city licenses. More than 100 foreign investors have invested in these companies. With a huge demand for bandwidth, domestic firms in partnership with international companies actively took part in competing with VSNL, MTNL and DoT in providing infrastructure and services (Gupta, 2001).

In March, 1999, the New Telecom Policy was announced. Its aim was to solve the legal dispute between DoT and TRAI. It promised to separate its service arm from its policy and licensing role (Gupta, 2001). India's continued telecommunications policy objective was to expand service availability to all parts of the country at affordable rates. As a part of this policy, in 2001, India decided to allow basic service license holders to use wireless technologies with limited mobility to compete in the market of providing local loop connections to subscribers. Moreover, private players have been allowed to provide international long distance services since April 2002 (Komandur, 2004).

The developments in the telecommunications sector in countries like India demonstrate that technology, political will, regulatory activism and market dynamics are the main drivers of the telecommunications market transformation (Komandur, 2004).

## Discussion

Government interventions in developing countries are usually pragmatic and flexible. Governments are repeatedly able to distance themselves from past policies that have failed or are no longer useful (Kim & Leipziger, 1993). The Chinese government has direct influence on the behaviour of state-owned operators while there are more private local firms penetrating the internet content sector than before. The government has continuously promoted the information society in many ways, and the primary development driver was to create a market-orientated environment for free competition spurred by gradual deregulation. From the case studies of China and Korea, it would seem that infrastructure building is generally market-driven under government control. However, it was really difficult to clearly separate the functions of government and enterprise management during the implementation process.

Here we can classify government actions in ICT infrastructure building as demand-supply or direct-indirect involvement (Yu, 2005). A number of roles for government in such a process are delineated in Figure 3.2. The linking and integrating functions in the matrix should not be overlooked and are in practice.

- *Role of sponsor* Start specific programmes on the supply side to meet strategic priorities. For example, the Chinese government made initial investments in CDMA and 3G technology.
- *Role of enabler* Encourage the application of e-infrastructure on the supply side. For example, public procurement of hardware, software and service has been implemented by the Chinese government annually.
- *Role of supporter* Encourage or stimulate development on the demand side without direct involvement. For example, internet education has been given to parts of the population including housewives, students and the elderly by local government.
- *Role of monitor* Supervise or direct the supply situation. For example, scope and quality of universal service was supervised nationally by the Chinese government.

We found that the roles of the government in the e-infrastructure evolution process changed at different stages. While the governments were directly involved in virtually every aspect of network building in the early days, they seem to play a more limited role afterwards, although they may decide to relinquish some of these responsibilities in the future. The government seems to continue to stimulate the

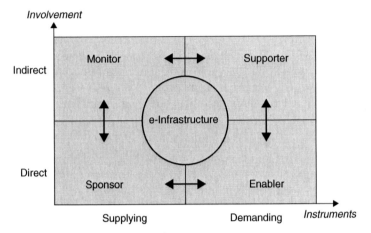

*Figure 3.2*   The role of the Chinese government in ICT industry development

development of information architecture in healthy new directions, if not to participate actively. Without substantial involvement by the government, however, it is impossible that the growth of information infrastructure will become a reality in countries with such large regional diversity as China.

## Summary

As a critical component within the reform of a national economy, the information and telecommunications sector has to follow the progress of macro changes which have taken place in a step-wise fashion in accordance with the principle of "act after trial". In a setting of limited and fragmented institutions such as this, regulation tends to be uncertain and unpredictable.

The large size of China's domestic market puts it in a favourable position to implement regulations and policies to encourage its indigenous industry base. The regulation and policy design for competitive markets of the future has actually stimulated the recent impressive growth of the ICT industry in China. Market structure tends to be more diversified and competition has been intensified. Hence competition has been created between state-owned telecommunications operators and limitations on foreign shares have been established to enable state-owned Chinese companies to assume a dominant position in the future marketplace.

An optimistic conclusion about the reform of the Chinese communications service is possible. But compared with current trends in world development, Chinese telecommunications reform has lagged behind and China is now still in transition to full competition. At the beginning of the twenty-first century, China's ICT sector remains largely state-controlled and competition in basic services is still between state-owned or state-run enterprises. The Chinese government still views the state-owned telecommunication operators as a combination of commercial, social and political arms of government. Two mobile operators must make profits for the government and at the same time receive market protection from government.

The driving forces behind the changing roles of regulations and laws come partly from the pressures surrounding China's entry into the WTO and partly from its long-term high-tech ambitions within economic globalization. Although the evolution of institutions in China is not driven by organizational competition, the interdependency between the changing institutions and the gradually more open economy will affect how local firms behave and exchange resources with others in order to attain greater competitive advantage. Such an institutional arrangement inevitably means that there will be some distorted behaviors and market uncertainties in future development. Both domestic and foreign players in this big emerging country therefore need to learn to navigate through the complex regulatory and legal environment in the ICT sectors.

# 4
# A Wireless China?

The greatest impact of mobile communications on access to communication services – in other words, increasing the number of people who are in reach of a telephone connection of any kind – can be seen in developing countries. In countries where mobile communications constitute the primary form of access, increased exchange of information on trade or health services is contributing to development goals; in countries where people commonly use both fixed-line and mobile communications, the personalized traits of the mobile phone are changing social interaction. (ITU, 2003)

## A miracle story?

A truly remarkable feature of telecommunications development performance in developing countries over the 1990s has been the widespread diffusion of the mobile telephone. In 1985, most developing countries had virtually no mobile telephony. By 1999, a number of countries, e.g. Cambodia and Venezuela, had more mobile subscribers than fixed-line subscribers (ITU, 2000).

Innovation in cellular mobile communications is characterized by a migration from Analogue to digital formats, a substitution of packet-switching for circuit-switching technologies, and continually increasing transmission speed or bandwidth. The wireless mobile market perhaps represents the most remarkable technology story of the past century; the extraordinary growth in mobile communication markets signals that mobile data broadband technologies can be both disruptive as a new channel as well as adding value to existing channels, by both enabling low cost access and increasing the reach of communications geographically. Mobile networks are characterized by high-cost, customized, engineering-intensive products and systems and the networks usually designed, implemented and configured for mobile operators are only produced by a small number of leading manufacturers who can provide the necessary specific facilities (Davies, 1997).

As the popularity of mobile data access grows, expert groups in both public institutions and private businesses are now speeding up efforts to create standards, technology and conditions that allow mobile network users to have access to multiple networks seamlessly at a very affordable price.

Latent consumer demands come forward to embrace new technology. There have been doubts about the rate of penetration of mobile telephony because of the convenience of fixed line telephones. But the greater convenience and freedom represented by mobiles have been the decisive factors in their rapid success in the world. Huge demand, albeit with variable requirements, has changed handsets from a high-tech image into fast moving modern consumer goods within a very short space of time. The industry is also unique in that companies have to be technology driven in the upstream of the value chain but at the same time fashion driven in the downstream. Highly active market demands have nurtured inventors, entrepreneurs, and even emerging countries like South Korea, Singapore, China, and now India. The market incubates the demands, then fosters entrepreneurs to engage with the globalized value chain.

In China, the remarkable growth of the mobile communications sector depends heavily on new innovations in technology and the continuous evolution of business models and applications. The evolution of the industry since its inception in 1987 appears to be an impressive industrial development process accompanied by market competition and policy intervention. This chapter will trace the stages of this development, capturing the patterns and drivers in this impressive process.

## Standardization and the technology of different generations

There is extensive literature on the relationship between industrial structure, entry to, and diffusion of different generation technology in, the telecommunications industry. A systemic innovation in the telecommunications sector requires a new standard, be it *de jure* or *de facto*, defining the overall framework of a new system, accompanied by a new set of interface specifications among component sub-systems. An important role of standardization in industrial innovation processes is to coordinate technical innovations performed independently by specialist companies and to synchronize them into an overall system framework, thereby assisting the creation of a new market.

In mobile telecommunications circles, examples of systemic innovation are, successively, first (1G), second (2G) and third generation (3G) systems. The timespan for developing a new cellular system was longer than 10 years and demanded access to a vast amount of resources. On the other hand, upgrading technology requires standardization bodies and government intervention.

In line with diffusion of innovation theory, the transformation of the mobile telecommunications market is the result of technology and service adoption by the users. The diffusion of innovation theory identifies four elements that characterize a successful diffusion process: 1) an innovation and its characteristics 2) that are communicated through specific channels 3) to the members of a social system 4) over time. General factors that have been found to influence adoption include adopter characteristics, the social network, the communication process, the characteristics of the promoters, and the innovation attributes. Attributes include testability, relative advantage, compatibility, observability and complexity (Rogers, 1995).

The cellular mobile industry has been entering a transition phase to 3G during the past decade. In 1999, the International Telecommunications Union (ITU) approved three industry standards for 3G wireless networks, comprising the so-called Universal Mobile Telecommunications System (UMTS). Based on CDMA technology, these three modes are commonly known as CDMA2000, WCDMA, and TD-SCDMA. The factors that determine a telecommunications operator to choose 3G development include not only the perceived or proven technological superiority of a particular standard, but also the politics, patents ownerships, and price. The EU parliament has mandated WCDMA as the European 3G standard. Various equipment vendors and network operators are progressing along alternative development paths in other regions of the world, including North America and East Asia (Dekleva, 2003).

## The evolution of China's mobile telecom industry

The evolution of China's mobile telecommunications industry since the end of the 1980s could be chronologically divided into four periods, namely the pure monopoly, competitive, pure duopoly and pre-3G periods.

### Pure monopoly period

The poorly-developed fixed telecommunications infrastructure in China has become a bottleneck for domestic economic growth in the past and the same story is repeated at the beginning of the mobile sector. The Total Access Communication System (TACS), the first analogue cellular system was provided monopolistically by China Telecom in Guangzhou, the biggest city in southern China. This first cellular exchange opened with a subscriber base of 150 in November 1987. The Advanced Mobile Phone System (AMPS) was originally introduced, also by China Telecom, in northwestern China. The heavy and clumsy analogue handset soon became a symbol of wealth and status in big cities due to high handset prices and service charges. In 1992, to purchase a handset from China Telecom (there was no other choice at that time) and to get connected, users incurred costs amounting to US$4,300, which was equivalent to fourteen times the GDP per capita in the same year (NBSC, 1992). Apparently, only local businessmen and foreign corporations were able to afford such mobile services.

Before 1998, China Telecom and the regulator of the telecommunications industry in China were affiliated. China Telecom was the only state-owned operator to monopolize the telecom market before the founding of its first competitor in 1994. As a regulator, the Ministry of Posts and Telecommunications (MPT) was also responsible for the operational and financial performance of China Telecom. In this respect, China Telecom and the MPT shared common interests (Xu, 2001). As a result, progress of competition in the mobile telecommunications market was impeded and the welfare of consumers could not be fully guaranteed. In 1993, the year when the Chinese government decided to establish a new competitor, there were less than 700,000 mobile phone subscribers in China, the world's most populous country.

## Competitive period

Facing the global trend towards liberalization and great pressures from home and abroad to break the monopoly, the Chinese government was inclined to use domestic competitors to pressure the mobile telecommunications sector to be more efficient. In July 1994, limited competition in the wireless service sector was finally introduced with the entry of China United Telecommunications Corporation (China Unicom), which is a joint venture between shareholders from the Ministry of Electronic Industry (MEI), the Ministry of Railways (MOR), and the Ministry of Electrical Power (MEP). The foundation of China Unicom formally indicated a fundamental paradigm shift in the evolution of the industry and ended the historical monopoly of the mobile telecommunications network in China.

China Unicom soon decided to launch an advanced digital mobile service to challenge the operation of the analogue network by China Telecom. On 17 July 1995, a year after its establishment, China Unicom launched its GSM (Global System for Mobile Communications) services commercially in Beijing, Shanghai, Tianjin and Guangzhou. At almost the same time, China Telecom also began to launch its GSM service, providing automatic roaming services to fifteen provinces and cities in January 1996. The analogue mobile subscribers of China Telecom reached 6.85 million in 1997 and then declined sharply. At the end of 2001, the analogue system was finally closed in China.

With the introduction of digital technology, increasing network capacities also stimulated the competition between the two mobile operators. China Telecom and China Unicom have been attracting customers by cutting the service prices, so customers have benefited from reduced handset prices and installation fees, shortened waiting lists and improved quality of service. The average price of an analogue handset, for example, was $3,300 in 1995, but the price of a digital handset in 1997 fell to $900 (*People's Daily*, 1997).

However, the MPT still enjoyed dual status as both regulator and dominant operator. This ineffective regulatory framework has put China Unicom at a competitive disadvantage, especially with respect to network interconnection (Xu, 2001). The service provision approval procedure by MPT limited network coverage. The number of its subscribers reached only 1.42 million in 1998. In the same year, China Unicom's revenue was only 0.89% of China Telecom's (MII, 1999). China Unicom and its shareholding ministries have made strong appeals for the restructuring of the regulatory institution, namely for complete functional and organizational separation between China Telecom and the regulator.

### Pure duopoly period

In April 1998, the Ministry of Information Industry (MII) was formally established by the State Council. MII enjoys a relatively neutral and independent status which enabled it to take a more pro-competitive stance in facilitating competition. As a result, China Mobile was separated from China Telecom, and has been specifically dedicated to mobile services since mid-1999.

Moreover, the attitude of the new regulator towards China Unicom also constituted a major change. Instead of limiting its development, MII made it a priority to facilitate the rapid growth of China Unicom. For instance, in 1999 MII initiated and completed a merger between China Unicom and GuoXin, a national radio paging company with total assets of RMB13 billion (US$1.6 billion). China Unicom also can provide GSM network services in any area with its master license without requiring special permission for each individual area as before. Furthermore, China Unicom has the right to have a 10% price float rate while the incumbent must obey the fixed tariff stipulated by the regulator.

As a result of this fundamental change in the regulatory environment, China Unicom has achieved rapid network expansion. With its aggressive marketing strategy, it has developed by leaps and bounds, not only in network size but also in the number of subscribers, since 1998. Its market share jumped from less than 6 per cent in 1998 to more than 33 per cent in 2002 (see Figure 4.1). A highly competitive telecommunications market structure has really emerged in China. Competition has been a strong catalyst for the volume development of the mobile communications market, especially since China Mobile and China Unicom launched the prepaid service without installation fee at the end of 1999. Installation fees charged to contracted mobile subscribers declined from $360–$610 in 1993 to $60–$70 in 1999 and were finally abolished in June 2001 (*People's Daily*, 2001).

Table 2.2 (see Chapter 2) shows the exponential growth of mobile subscribers in China since China Unicom entered the market.

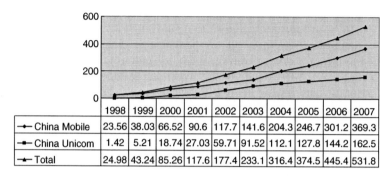

| | 1998 | 1999 | 2000 | 2001 | 2002 | 2003 | 2004 | 2005 | 2006 | 2007 |
|---|---|---|---|---|---|---|---|---|---|---|
| China Mobile | 23.56 | 38.03 | 66.52 | 90.6 | 117.7 | 141.6 | 204.3 | 246.7 | 301.2 | 369.3 |
| China Unicom | 1.42 | 5.21 | 18.74 | 27.03 | 59.71 | 91.52 | 112.1 | 127.8 | 144.2 | 162.5 |
| Total | 24.98 | 43.24 | 85.26 | 117.6 | 177.4 | 233.1 | 316.4 | 374.5 | 445.4 | 531.8 |

*Figure 4.1* Growth of wireless telecom subscribers in China
*Source*: MII, CCID.

In accordance with the decision of the State Council, MII granted a license for Code Division Multiple Access (CDMA) exclusively to China Unicom in 1999. China Unicom signed a CDMA Intellectual Property Agreement with Qualcomm Inc. in February 2000 and finally launched its CDMA IS-95A network in January 2002. Now China Unicom has become the only venture in the world which runs both GSM and CDMA networks. Despite the challenges of running two brand names and keeping two sets of engineering, marketing and sales forces, figures from China Unicom indicated that by the end of 2002, it had recruited some 61.2 million GSM subscribers and over 7 million CDMA IS-95A subscribers. Its CDMA IS-95A network tended to provide additional wireless data service, targeting medium and high-end subscribers, while the GSM network was concentrating on low-end subscribers who only favour voice transmission services.

In order to fully explore the potential of the network resources and to generate more revenue from their current subscriber base, both China Mobile and China Unicom have introduced a variety of value-added services in the past years. These services include caller number display, voicemail, short messages, call forwarding, call waiting, third party call and VoIP long distance call. At the end of 2002, subscribers of China Mobile and China Unicom totalled a remarkable 206.3 million. In the same year the annual revenue of these two mobile operators reached US$24.5 billion.

We can see that the decision to introduce GSM and CDMA IS-95A standards in China, in turn, a period of rapid incremental progress. The mobile penetration rate in China grew from 0.05% in 1993 to 16.16% in 2002 (MII, 2002). To further explore the mobile data market and make up for their sharply declining ARPU (Average Revenue per User) indicator, China Mobile and China Unicom formally launched their nation-wide WAP (Wireless Application Protocol) service in May 2000. In November 2000, China Mobile introduced the Monternet program, which combines the platform for mobile and internet. Under this program, mobile data service providers can access the mobile network anywhere to provide nationwide service. Such services include messaging, phone payment, mobile QQ, mobile securities, mobile location and broadband services. China Mobile keeps 9% of the traffic revenues, with the information service providers receiving 91%.

Faced with the global trends in the mobile data business, in the last quarter of 2000 China Mobile set up a subsidiary to support the Monternet program in partnership with HP Corp. In the meantime, China Unicom also began to provide mobile data services to fuel the growth of its service revenue. It formed a joint venture with Qualcomm Inc. in February 2003 to explore the mobile data market, boosting the development of its CDMA wireless data applications through BREW (Binary Runtime Environment for Wireless) platforms.

### The popularity of SMS

The success of SMS is largely a result of its low cost and convenience, and the Chinese user's cultural traditions (Sangwan & Pau, 2005). Currently, SMS is limited to a maximum of 160 characters in the display screen, but it is an economical and cost-effective way to communicate. In 2004 Chinese mobile phones users sent 217.76 billion short messages, up 58.8% from the previous year (*China Daily*, 2005). China's two largest mobile telecommunications operators, China Mobile and China Unicom, were expected to handle a total of 550 billion text messages in 2004 (Pienaar, 2004). On average, each user spends RMB21 (US$2.57) on SMS per month, excluding the revenue generated by content providers. The above numbers, however, are only estimates, as the dominant prepaid service bundles actually use an SMS price which is lower – up to 40% according to some estimates.

Interestingly, some leading wire-line internet portals like SINA.com and Sohu.com also allow users to send SMS via their PCs to the handsets of mobile phone users. In addition to SMS chatting, guessing games, news alerts and information inquiries, other innovative personalized services, such as reading literature, are projected to be a success in the Chinese market. The service enables mobile phones users to read a piece of literature by receiving an episode of the user's choice in a SMS message every day, costing about RMB 0.30 (US$ 0.04) each (*China Daily*, 2005). It has become an important section of these mobile portals.

Mobile operators and service providers are discovering that they can also profit from the information services based on SMS content provided by insurers, security firms, banks, airlines, and shopping malls. The joint SMS centre, called MOBNIC (Mobile Network Information Centre), launched in 2005 by China Mobile, China Unicom, the China Mobile Communication Association and other service providers enables users to visit various "SMS-based servers". The mobile users can send a specific number or code via an SMS message to access the "SMS server" to retrieve interactive information services. SMS centres offer small and medium-sized enterprises a channel to access their markets more cheaply and conveniently.

China is not immune from the worldwide trend away from mobile voice to mobile data. On the other side, and in the light of the decreasing ARPU in voice communications, operators are eager to explore new revenue streams other than traditional voice services. Some new value-added services like location-based service, mobile payment, mobile TV, wireless music and mobile email are emerging as the business opportunities of the future. They will become increasingly important in the mobile service portfolio of the mobile operators.

## Towards 3G and beyond

At the beginning of the new century, faced with the global emerging tide of 3G, China Mobile began to aggressively upgrade its GSM network system facilities to GPRS networks. In May 2002, it launched its GPRS service commercially in China's principal cities. To respond to the technological challenge posed by China Mobile, China Unicom began upgrading the existing CDMA-IS95A network to a CDMA2000-1X network. The CDMA2000-1X service was first introduced in

Shanghai in January 2003. In 2004 China Unicom also launched a dual-mode handset that is capable of supporting both the GSM and CDMA systems under the new brand.

The wireless market is characterized by changing end-user preferences and demand for new and advanced functions and applications on wireless handsets. Since many 3G applications can be made available via GPRS and CDMA2000-1X networks, the lessons and experiences learnt from these transitional networks would be beneficial not only to the two mobile operators but also to value-added service providers, and will impact 3G development in the longer term in China. Therefore, the regulator and the two existing operators need to do intensive and careful studies on the synchronization between the technologies and market of the future before making a decision.

## Indigenous innovation: China's 3G standardization

Developing proprietary systems to gain technological advantages has been recognized as a strategic priority by Chinese policy makers (Suttmeier, 2005). As early as 1997, the vice president of CATT (China Academy of Telecommunications Technology)and his team were exploring SCDMA radio access technology in Beijing. To respond to the ITU (International Telecommunications Union) proposals for potential 3G standards, the MPT (Ministry of Posts and Telecommunications) established a 3G Transmission Technology Assessment and Coordination Group, composed of leading institutes and operators in China in July 1997, and registered with the ITU as the eleventh assessment group.

In January 1998, the MPT held a conference in Beijing to prepare for China's 3G proposal. There were fierce disagreements on whether China should submit its own proposal for 3G standards, a domain in which the developed countries usually set the game rules. The MPT conference finally decided to submit China's 3G proposal (Dong *et al.*, 2006) and after several months of hard work, Dr. Li's team brought out the TD-SCDMA technology scheme (People's P&T, 2003). In June 1998, the TD-SCDMA proposal was submitted to the ITU for evaluation by CATT on behalf of the Chinese government. This initiative was signed by the Minister of the MPT and supported by Siemens (Dong *et al.*, 2006; Li, 2000).

In May 2000, TD-SCDMA was accepted as one of the three formal 3G transmission standards at the ITU World Radio Conference (WRC) in Istanbul, together with CDMA2000 and W-CDMA standards. On 16 March 2001, at its eleventh plenary session, TD-SCDMA was formally accepted by 3GPP (Third Generation Partnership Project), which is a consortium of industrial members, as part of UMTS Release 4 (ITU, 2002). This meant that TD-SCDMA had also been accepted by the industry internationally as a possible option for global 3G deployment (Wang, 2001). In this way it became an internationally recognized standard, which could be used in different kinds of radio deployment scenarios: from rural to dense urban areas, for pedestrians and people on the move. As the first proposed internationally accepted telecommunications platform standard, TD-SCDMA was considered a key milestone for the development of Chinese high-tech industry (Zhang, 2000). One senior member of the CATT staff who participated in the standards proposal recalled:

> *Some people don't believe China as a developing country can propose an international 3G standard. But the domestic industry realizes that it must have its first attempt in such a strategic sector. The MPT officials and industry experts worked together during the whole TD-SCDMA proposal preparation. CATT as a national institute has played a key role in this process. But frankly, we haven't expected that there will be so many hard and complex issues to build an indigenous 3G industry following the acceptance of TD-SCDMA standard by ITU. (Interview at China Academy of Telecom Research)*

Three main *de facto* 3G standards were accepted by ITU in 2000, wideband CDMA (WCDMA) proposed by Europe, CDMA2000 by the United States, and TD-SCDMA by China. The WCDMA standard has been adopted by most European and Asian mobile operators and developed by global vendors such as Ericsson, Nokia and Motorola, while CDMA2000 is a standard developed by Qualcomm Inc. and backed by foreign firms such as Lucent and Motorola. TD-SCDMA standard is widely perceived as a latecomer and the least mature of the three competing 3G technologies, though it offers several new functions like flexible spectrum allocation (Meng & Yao, 2000).

Before 2001, TD-SCDMA was neglected by most MNCs and only Siemens from Germany established a strategic alliance with Datang to support TD-SCDMA (Dong *et al.*, 2006). The two domestic mobile operators, China Mobile and China Unicom, were in fierce competition with each other, upgrading their existing networks. Since the WCDMA and CDMA2000 standards were considered as their natural technological choice, based on their existing networks, they showed little interest in the home-grown standard during this period.

### April 2001–February 2004: verification and development

After the legitimization of the TD-SCDMA standard, the Chinese government and domestic vendors were faced with a lot of work testing and commercializing this as yet unproven indigenous technology. Datang, the standard sponsor, recognized that in the development of a new generation mobile system, the effective integration of different key technologies, including microprocessors, radio, switching and testing technologies is critical. However, Datang lacked the experience of system architecture development and key components such as terminal chipsets. Hence some R&D activities in the chipset area were mostly outsourced to its joint ventures with Samsung, Philips, Texas Instruments and other partners.

In April 2001, the first call between a TD-SCDMA base station simulator and a field system was successfully trialled in Beijing, which validated the technical feasibility of the home-grown standard. In March 2002, Datang Mobile Corporation was established by the Datang Group. Datang Mobile would specialize in the standardization of TD-SCDMA. It should be pointed out that on 1 October 2001, Japan's NTT DoCoMo also commercially launched the first 3G network in the world based on WCDMA, starting the era of global 3G mobile telecommunications. NEC, Ericsson and other global vendors had already received some commercial orders for WCDMA network deployment.

For a long time, major international vendors, as well as new domestic entrants like ZTE and Huawei, had been making efforts to establish WCDMA R&D facilities in China. During this period, most foreign vendors adopted the "wait and see" strategy on China's TD-SCDMA standard. Incumbent telecommunications operators like China Mobile and China Unicom were interested in adopting the WCDMA or CDMA2000 standards, which were market-proven in Europe and Asia. By contrast, TD-SCDMA was seen as an immature technical option in terms of service profitability and technological compatibility with the rest of the world.

In view of the fact that development of the TD-SCDMA system was far behind the other two international standards in terms of commercial advancement, the government decided to become actively involved in standardization. On 23 October 2002, MII published the TD-SCDMA frequency spectrum plan and assigned a total of 155MHz asymmetrical frequencies to the TD-SCDMA standard, compared with the 60 MHz bandwidth allocated to WCDMA and CDMA2000 spectrum, respectively to each. This move sent a strong policy signal to those domestic firms without an interest in TD-SCDMA. The TDIA (TD-SCDMA Industry Alliance) was established in the same month by MII, with eight founding domestic members. Huawei, ZTE and Putian, three leading domestic firms, formally aligned with Datang, and as a result, the TD-SCDMA industrialization process became more structured.

In January 2003, Philips, Datang and Samsung Electronics formed a joint venture company named T3G to design and license core cellular TD-SCDMA chipsets and reference designs, with Motorola joining later. In November 2003, supported by the government, Datang transferred key IPRs of the TD-SCDMA wireless system to Putian and ZTE, two leading domestic vendors in China. A senior manager at Putian commented:

> The transfer of key TD-SCDMA IPRs and knowledge from Datang is critical for Putian and ZTE to actively participate in the TD-SCDMA development. The transfer enables us to quickly approach the product development frontiers and thus we needn't start from scratch. This has really quickened the whole standardization process. At the firm level, we have soon transformed our R&D orientation from WCDMA to TD-SCDMA. (Interview with Putian).

In February 2004, the National Development and Reform Commission (NDRC), the ministry responsible for formulating policies for economic and social development and leading overall economic system restructuring, the Ministry of Sciences and Technology (MOST) and MII launched TRIP (TD-SCDMA R&D and Industrialization Programme) to subsidize domestic firms in their R&D activities. The overall programme budget was RMB 708 million ($85.4 million). This

R&D subsidy aimed to further the standardization process, and each indigenous firm favouring the TD-SCDMA standard was eligible to share part of this financial support. As a result, TD-SCDMA standardization finally stepped into the fast lane (Zhang, 2008). During this period, attracting more heavyweight playersto become involved in home-grown standards development and implementation became the strategic priority of the government.

### February 2004–March 2007: industrialization

The TRIP programme, sponsored by three ministries, speeded up the whole industrialization process and attracted resources input by other domestic firms. For example, ZTE's TD-SCDMA research staff soon reached 3,000. ZTE rolled out their TD-SCDMA wireless subsystem soon after the TRIP programme was launched. In November 2004, MII decided to launch the TD-SCDMA industrialization network test which aimed to create commercial prototypes of TD-SCDMA wireless subsystems (Zhang, 2008).

However, the underdevelopment and instability of products delayed the whole TD-SCDMA commercialization progress (Wang, 2004). As the TD-SCDMA sponsor, Datang had to co-develop with chipset firms to break the development bottleneck of TD-SCDMA terminal chipsets. Spreadtrum, the leading Chinese semiconductor firm launched by overseas returnees, developed the first TD-SCDMA terminal chipset in April 2004. Subsequently, with the support of T3G, Samsung developed the first GSM/TD-SCDMA dual module terminal in December 2004. LG and the other indigenous handset manufacturers successfully developed TD-SCDMA terminal prototypes.

In December 2005, the vice minister of MII announced that with the maturing of the core technology and the formation of the TD-SCDMA industrial chain, TD-SCDMA would play an important role in the future 3G landscape and some leading national operators would be granted TD-SCDMA licenses (Forbes, 2005). With continued government support, the development of the TD-SCDMA system witnessed rapid progress and the main system development work was finished by the end of 2005. The industrial chain of TD-SCDMA covering areas of technical standards, wireless systems, core networks, chipsets, terminals and testing equipments also took shape. On 20 January 2006, in recognition of the technological and commercial feasibility of the home-grown standard, MII announced TD-SCDMA as the first 3G national technology standard to be adopted by China. At the same time, twenty-three technological specifications for TD-SCDMA handsets, radio access equipment and wireless interface were published to facilitate development in domestic and foreign firms (MII, 2006).

At this stage, some foreign vendors began to realize that they could not afford to miss out on the design of the China's TD-SCDMA infrastructure, which might affect their future market share. Recognizing the possible prevalence of China's 3G standard, the major foreign vendors Alcatel, Ericsson, and Nokia have established different strategic alliances supporting TD-SCDMA with the Chinese firms Datang, ZTE and Putian respectively since the end of 2004. Siemens announced a new joint venture with Huawei in 2005 (Wang, 2005). Some foreign vendors began to strategically engage in the TD-SCDMA commercialization process. For example, Alcatel's core network technology will be integrated into Datang's TD-SCDMA solution and the industrialization of Datang's wireless stations will also be carried out in Alcatel.

Since 2004, more domestic and foreign players had become actively involved in TD-SCDMA standardization with their specific complementary assets (e.g., manufacturing, marketing, distribution channels). A multi-vendor and multi-national environment essential for the development of TD-SCDMA finally emerged with increasing commercial advancement and inter-organizational collaboration over time. MII arranged for the four national telecommunications operators including China Mobile, China Unicom, China Telecom and China Netcom to take part in commercial field testing and Datang, Nortel, Putian, and ZTE established two TD-SCDMA trial networks in Beijing and Shanghai, respectively. Interoperability testing of different equipment was carried out and the standards-based chipsets, software and support systems were also finalized.

In December 2004, the world's first TD-SCDMA international call was made from Datang's Beijing laboratory to the Chinese Prime Minister on a visit to the Netherlands, which demonstrated firm support from central government (Dong *et al.*, 2006). At the same time, domestic vendors were grasping the main intellectual property rights (IPR) of TD-SCDMA technology. By the beginning of 2007, a total of 309 key TD-SCDMA patents had been formally filed in the State Intellectual Property Office (SIPO), and most of them are owned by domestic vendors like ZTE and Datang (CIPS, 2007).

In February 2007, SK Telecom of South Korea signed a collaboration contract with China's NDRC ministry to establish a TD-SCDMA project in Korea. On 10 April 2007, during a visit to Korea, China's Prime Minister made a TD-SCDMA video phone call to the MII minister in Beijing (Li, 2007). The Vice Chief Engineer of China Mobile was appointed as Chairman of Datang in May 2006 in order to support future collaboration between the key domestic operators and domestic vendors. In August 2006 the MII and Ministry of Personnel (MOP) held a TD-SCDMA Senior Training Course for the main industrial administrators and operator executives to promote understanding of the advantages of TD-SCDMA (Zhou, 2007).

Globally, WCDMA has taken off and become the leading 3G standard since 2005. Forty WCDMA networks launched commercial services during 2005 and there were over 55 million WCDMA subscribers by the end of March 2006 (GSA, 2006). In this global context, some branches of China Mobile deployed the WCDMA trial network in several cities in 2005, but then were closed under pressure from MII (Li & Shi, 2006). On the other hand, operating risks decreased with widespread availability of TD-SCDMA devices at the end of 2006. The role of those Chinese operators who were still reluctant to engage with TD-SCDMA became critical. As TD-SCDMA standardization was apparently progressing more slowly than originally planned, the government took a hard line in strongly requiring the implementation of indigenous 3G standards. Faced with increasing pressure from central government to launch home-grown standards for the Beijing Olympics, China Mobile as the biggest state-owned operator finally had to jump onto the chariot of TD-SCDMA.

### March 2007: enforcement and further evolution

The 2008 Beijing Olympic Games were approaching. China wanted to use them as an opportunity to showcase its economic and technological achievements. On the other hand, the Olympic Games also created enormous market demands for 3G mobile multimedia technology, and the government set a deadline for China Mobile to offer TD-SCDMA-based services.

In March 2007, China Mobile, a partner of Beijing 2008 Olympics with nearly 400 million mobile users, began to deploy a TD-SCDMA pilot network in eight cities (Colin, 2007). On 1 April 2008, the network began commercial trials and started to provide new

Olympics-focused services, such as video-telephone and mobile TV, in Beijing and seven other cities. Later, in July 2008, China Mobile formally joined the TD-SCDMA alliance, making it the first incumbent operator of this alliance (Liu, 2008). According to the official Xinhua agency, by the end of the Beijing Olympics in late August, TD-SCDMA users of China Mobile had reached 175,000. 3G networks would soon be deployed in 38 cities (www.gov.cn, website).

### Leading to 4G

During the gradual commercialization of 3G systems, research on 4G mobile communications had already begun. In China, a B3G beyond third generation) research programme, the Future Technologies for a Universal Radio Environment (FuTURE) project, is listed in the 863 Programme of China's Science and Technology Development Plan in the Tenth Five Years, formally starting in 2002. The goal of the project is to support theoretical research and evaluation of proposed technologies for B3G mobile communications. At the same time, some leading companies like Huawei and research institutions like CAS have also begun their own B3G research.

Yet just as TD-CDMA is ready to establish itself with mobile broadband services in China, it faces the prospect of being made redundant by the rapid global entry to the market of WCDMA leading to *High-speed Down Link Packet Access* (HSDPA) mobile standards. TD-HSDPA (3.5G TD-SCDMA based HSDPA) utilizes existing network investments, enabling the domestic TD-SCDMA to cater for everything from mobile voice telephony, video telephony, mobile TV and mobile broadband to laptops, and now also fixed services with ADSL speed. The first single chip supported TD-HSDPA was launched in February 2007 by Spreadtrum.

### PHS and WLAN

*Xiaolingtong* (meaning "little smart" in Chinese and abbreviated as XLT) is a new type of wireless mobile phone system developed in China, based on the Personal Handy Phone System (PHS) technology that originated in Japan in 1995. Connecting to existing fixed-line telephone networks through micro-cell radio, it provides mobile wireless access to ordinary local Public Switched Telephone Network (PSTN) services. By providing low-cost outgoing calls and free incoming calls, XLT services have experienced very rapid growth in China. From its 1998 launch in Yuhang, a small city in Zhejiang province, XLT has spread to more than 600 cities nationwide with subscribers reaching nearly 80 million in June 2005 (CCID, 2005).

Besides voice communication, XLT can provide data transmission and a variety of value-added services such as short message service (SMS), internet access, downloading of pictures and ringtones. The introduction of XLT in China, however, has not been smooth. It has been accompanied by much criticism and suspicion about its survival and future growth.

### Characteristics of the emerging innovation

XLT or PAS (personal access phone system) is a new personal wireless access phone system. It uses micro-cellular technology to provide wireless services based on the fixed-line network. The advantages of XLT are:

a) XLT provides voice communications equivalent to that of existing wired telephone systems.
b) XLT adopts the fixed telephony fee standard: the monthly rental is 25 US dollars, and the call charge is 3+1 (0.2 dollars the first 3 minutes, 0.1 dollars per minute after the first 3 minutes). Charges are one-way.
c) The low radiation and low levels of electronic interference.

However, the disadvantages of XLT are:

a) XLT has limitations in terms of roaming capability, and usually provides mobility within local metropolitan areas.
b) Because of the low power input, the signal overlay of XLT is less than that of mobile telephones, and the network improvements need constant adjustment.Initially, customers can experience intermittent signal and, in some places, even no signal.

### Facilitating market demand, carriers and equipment manufacturers

There is some imbalance in the development of China's wireless telecommunications industry. Competition is increasingly vigorous at the top end of the market, leading to saturation, whereas there is a great deal of unmet demand at the lower end of the market.

According to statistics for the end of 1999, there were 43,300,000 (MII, 1999) mobile subscribers in China, about 4% of the national population. There was a huge business opportunity in the form of a major unmet wireless demand from middle-income and salaried groups, which accounted for more than 50% of the national population.

In response to market demand, UTStarcom Inc., an IT service business company, introduced the Japanese PHS technology and then entered the wireless access network trial managed by the MPT in August 1996. XLT, launched in Yuhang December 1997, was the complement and extension of fixed-line networks, merging wireless access technology with fixed-line networks for the first time XLT creates local access from fixed-line to wireless and can channel a huge traffic flow, providing a new cheap wireless telecommunication service.

Cost saving is the key driver for new technology diffusion and XLT has the advantage of low cost. Unlike PHS, XLT provides local users with wireless access by fully utilizing idle fixed network resources, using international standard V5 to connect PSTN switches. The cost of the project is only 1/5 of the Japanese PHS system, and can reduce as networks grow. The Japanese PHS, based on independent mobile systems, needs the whole switch machine, network and operation maintenance system, so its costs are comparatively high. Because XLT makes use of the idle fixed network resources, the costs are quite low. One-way charges, together with cheap phones, considerably reduce the expense of wireless communication, and the target markets of XLT, correspondingly, are salaried groups, especially middle- and low-level users who are less mobile.

### Policy design and implementation

In January 1998, the MII allowed Yuhang city to launch XLT operations. At the time XLT was forbidden in big cities, operation only being permitted in medium-sized and small cities.

In June 2000, the MII issued a circular on criteria for PHS construction and operation (MII document 604), which confirmed XLT as the complement and extension of fixed-line network services, and legalized it as "small scope, low speed and wireless access", the application of which was limited to voice and data communication services in small cities and villages, and forbidden in big cities. Document 604 regulated the basic principles and scope of XLT for the first time in China, formalising its legal position: XLT is the complement and extension of fixed-line network services belonging to fixed-line telephony services, but not mobile telephony services. XLT therefore adopts fixed-line telephony fee standards and one-way charges, and these give XLT the opportunity of diffusion and expansion. However, the geographical restriction on XLT remained. After XLT had been legalized, China Telecom and China Mobile developed XLT services, growing their businesses in succession. In 1999, there were only seven cities providing XLT services. In August 2000, there were more than sixty.

However, faced with the rapid development of XLT, and in order not to breach public mobile market competition orders, another document was issued by MII in November 2000, requesting local telecommunications companies to raise the service charge. In September 2002, it was clear that, as regulated by MII, XLT had not been restricted except for Beijing and Shanghai cities.

During the National People's Congress and the Chinese People's Political Consultative Conference in 2002, the Minister of MII openly said that the government's attitude to XLT was neither to support, nor constrain. It was thus clear that there was no barrier to XLT. In March 2003, XLT was introduced in one district of Beijing. In April, it was formally used in Guangzhou City. On 17 May 2004, XLT entered the central zone in Beijing, and at the same time, XLT appeared in business application in Shanghai.

At the end of 2004, with intervenion from the MII, XLT's short message service was able to intercommunicate with China Mobile and China Unicom, the two main incumbent competitors. With the short message service interconnecting with China Telecom and China Netcom, as well as with Mobile and Unicom, and with the issue of the Private Ring Back Tone and wireless internet services, XLT's value-added services had been developed.

### The consequences of diffusion

By October 2005, XLT had appeared in 400 cities in China, and the number of XLT users exceeded 85 million. China became the biggest XLT market in the world (MII, 2005). Figure 4.2 shows the growth of subscriber numbers.

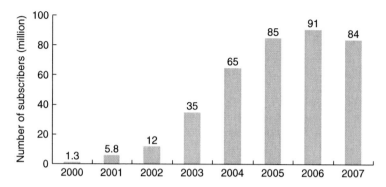

*Figure 4.2*  Growth of subscribers of XLT in China
*Source*: MII.

XLT entered the wireless communication market in response to demand, triggering tremendous competition, changing people's attitude to consumption, and causing the wireless market to flourish. The number of mobile users is still increasing

At the end of 2002, China Mobile had the biggest telecom income, with a 37.4% share, and it consolidated its ascendant position throughout 2003 and 2004. With China Mobile's GSM, China Unicom's GSM and CDMA, and XLT, tripartite competition gradually arose in the mobile market (see Figure 4.3). In the face of competitive press from XLT, the price of mobile communications came down, and the service level improved, furthering development of the wireless sector. China Mobile and China Unicom had to pay more attention to improving quality of service, adopting new technology and introducing new services. The biggest contribution of XLT was that it broke the monopoly in the wireless field, promoted competition in the mobile communications market.

It should be noticed that in 2005, with the approach of 3G, the fixed network carriers reduced their investment in XLT networks. Meanwhile, with mobile service tariffs reducing, the price advantage of XLT was not obvious. The number of XLT subscribers reached a peak of 93,410,000 and then began to fall. The role of XLT changed from replacing mobile service to being replaced by mobile service.

Another technology currently operating at the margins of the market is the Wireless Local Access Network (WLAN). With limited market

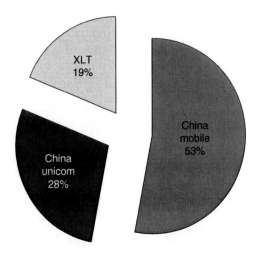

*Figure 4.3*   The market share of two mobile operators and XLT (2005)

for the time being, WLAN still has some potential to influence the mobile market. From the regulatory perspective, WLAN benefits from the same treatment as in other parts of the world: it is currently un-regulated. This status can be attributed to the emerging nature of the technology (not yet on the regulator's radar screen) rather than a positive decision from the Chinese regulator to leave WLAN outside its regulatory scope. The disruptive nature of WLAN is exemplified by the issuing of standards forcing foreign manufacturers to cooperate with domestic companies to produce WLAN equipment in 2004.

## A future wireless China?

Usually mobile phones in less developed economies are playing the same crucial role that fixed telephony played in the richer economies in the 1970s and 1980s. Mobile phones substitute for fixed lines in poor countries, but complement fixed lines in rich countries, implying that they have a stronger growth impact in poor countries. Many countries with under-developed fixed-line networks have achieved rapid mobile telephone growth with much less investment than fixed-line networks would have needed (Waverman *et al.*, 2005).

Differences in the penetration and diffusion of mobile telephones may explain some of the differences in growth rates between developing countries. During the past decade, the cellular mobile telecommunication and the internet industries have both grown explosively in China. These two technologies are having increasing impacts not only on people's daily life, but also on the way business is conducted. Mobile telephones started as a premium service, offering voice transmission with the benefit of mobility. Extended by the dynamics of technology and cost, mobile communication is now evolving into a more mature and widespread service offering both voice and data services. The foundation of China's information society will undoubtedly be its mobile infrastructure.

# 5
# The Rise of Indigenous Firms: Emerging Global Stars

## Introduction

Globalization, or internationalization, is defined as "the process of increasing involvement in international operations" (Welch & Luostarinen, 1988). A firm's positioning strategy becomes more and more essential in the context of globalization. It is vital, in terms of value creation and appropriation, for firms coming late to the market to clearly define their mission and identify their strengths. At the same time, however, industrial dynamics also play a critical role. Dynamically monitoring position and making wise moves are critical factors that directly relate to survival and growth.

The underlying factors and dynamics encouraging latecomer firms to sell goods or services in foreign markets are not well understood. In addition, relatively little research has been conducted to explore whether the propensity to export abroad enhances a firm's subsequent size and performance in a developing context. According to Jansson (2007), we are about to experience "the third wave of internationalization". The first wave was the internationalization of big companies from Europe and North America, which took place from the end of the nineteenth century until the 1970s, a process that mainly involved market economies in Europe and North America. The second wave was that of companies from Japan and later South Korea, which mainly took place from the 1960s until the 1990s. These companies emerged on the world market while Western companies simultaneously expanded into East Asia. The third wave involves companies from mature Western markets establishing themselves in China,

India, Russia, and central and eastern Europe (CEE), while companies from these countries are entering the world market and in some cases themselves becoming MNCs. This has been the result of the opening up of China and India to international markets as well as the integration of the CEE countries into the common market of the EU.

China is emerging as a country of rapidly growing importance in global trade. The Chinese economy has undergone a transformation from an extremely inward-oriented economy without market incentives to an economy that is deeply integrated into the world economy. Some leading firms are trying to combine Western professional management practices with the wisdom of Eastern culture and this phenomenon is especially apparent in the ICT area.

After years of hard work, several leading Chinese firms across different sectors are becoming more and more internationalized in their operations. Some of them are trying to establish a global operating network, attaching great importance to being as close as possible to local customers in foreign markets. They are eager to transform from marginal players to core contributors in global platforms. Some typical examples, which we will discuss in more detail, are Huawei, Lenovo, ZTE,TCL, Sina, Alibaba and Spreadtrum,

Many Chinese companies tend to internationalize and reposition themselves from the low to high price sector as they either discover that their home market in the high-price sector is not big enough or as they realize that tough local competition will present a barrier to large volumes and profits (Brouthers & Xu, 2002). Companies repositioning have come to the conclusion that they can reach equal or larger total profits in the high price/low volume sector than in low price sectors with larger volumes. The higher price levels and thus potential for higher margins in Western countries become very attractive for companies either in the process of, or considering, strategic repositioning.

A strategy of cost leading results in superior performance. However, performance satisfaction has increased when exporters in the developing countries have used a branding product strategy. Some companies will reposition to the high price/low volume sector with the view of potentially increasing their total profit in these high price sectors. In doing so, they lose the strategic advantage of their home country conditions (Brouthers & Xu, 2002). Chinese companies can also benefit from their lower costs in the high price/high value sectors. They have a cost advantage compared to Western companies in terms of lower hourly rates in R&D and product development, lower capital costs and an overall lower cost structure. This gives them a potential for higher margins in high price sectors compared with Western companies. However, when targeting Western countries, part of this cost advantage is constrained because of a need to invest in securing assets that they lack domestically and that are fundamental in the high price/high value sectors. Such strategic assets are, for example, international branding, parts of R&D, internationally experienced management and local support, which can never be neglected when aiming for the high price/high value sectors (Soderman *et al.*, 2008). China's labour cost advantage is vanishing as other Asian countries become significantly more cost-competitive and as fierce domestic competition in China continues to suppress profits.

## Huawei

### Profile of Huawei

Established in 1988 initially as a private trading company in Southern China, Huawei Technologies later entered the telecommunications manufacturing industry. From the very beginning, Huawei has aimed to build a world-class and technologically advanced telecom-equipment manufacturer. Now it is a leading high-tech enterprise which specializes in R&D, production and marketing of communications equipment, providing customized network solutions for telecommunication carriers in the optical, fixed, mobile and data communication sectors. Huawei's products and solutions encompass wireless products, core network products, network products, applications and software, as well as terminals.

Huawei has developed soundly during the past 10 years in terms of turnover, human resources and global expansion. With nearly 10,000 R&D personnel, Huawei became a global player and ranked sixteenth among the top telecommunications manufacturers in the world (IDATE, 2002). The company is committed to providing innovative and customized products, services and solutions to create long-term value and growth potential for its customers. Its international contract sales leapt six-fold, from $244 million in 2001, then 11% of total revenues, to $2.28 billion in 2004 – 41% of total contract sales of $5.58 billion. A milestone was reached in April 2005, when BT (British Telecommunications plc), one of the leading global operators, selected Huawei as one of its preferred suppliers of communications equipment for a £10 billion upgrade of its network (Light Reading, 2005). Most of Huawei's products are designed based on Huawei's ASIC chipset and utilize shared platforms to provide quality and cost-effective products.

Huawei Technologies has become a leader in providing next generation telecommunications networks and now serves 31 of the world's top 50 operators, along with over one billion users worldwide. By the end of 2006, Huawei had 61,909 employees spreading across China and more than 40 other countries, of whom 48% were dedicated to R&D. Huawei's global R&D centres are located in Bangalore in India, Silicon Valley and Dallas in the US, Stockholm in Sweden and Moscow in Russia in addition to those in Beijing, Shanghai, Nanjing, Shenzhen, Hangzhou and Chengdu in China (Huawei website, 2008). Table 5.1 shows Huawei's corporate evolution.

*Table 5.1*   Corporate evolution process of Huawei

|  | 2002 | 2003 | 2004 | 2005 | 2006 | 2007 |
|---|---|---|---|---|---|---|
| Turnover ($ billion) | 2.7 | 3.8 | 5.6 | 8.2 | 11.0 | 16.0 |
| Number of employees | 20,000 | 20,000 | 3,0000 | 37,000 | 62,000 | 65,000 |
| Overseas sales (RMB billion) | 0.6 | 1.1 | 2.3 | 4.8 | 7.2 | 11.5 |

*Source*: CCID, authors' interview.

Soon after the founding of the firm, Huawei identified the great potential of the telecom switching market in China. In 1990, it began to devote its main R&D resources to the development of SPC switching products. As a latecomer, Huawei apparently could not afford the risks of developing a whole new system from scratch. By examining existing foreign systems, Huawei basically grasped the design technology of the system architecture and related software design technology. Afterwards, Huawei successfully developed its primary version of C&C08A (2,000 lines capacity) switching at the beginning of 1993.

At that time, MNCs were only focusing their resources on the high end of the local market – the large cities and the urban business users – while Huawei paid more attention to the vast hinterlands like small cities and counties. However, the lack of network operation experience was a deficit which Huawei had to make up quickly. It was very difficult for incumbent telecommunications operators to cooperate in network trials with a local newcomer. In 1993, several county-level telecom corporations in Zhejiang province finally agreed to operate Huawei's primary C&C08A systems, which demonstrated that all the equipment performed as well as promised (Yu, 2006). Huawei began to build its brand reputation in the local telecommunications market and quickly penetrated into most county-level markets.

The initial success in primary SPC switches provided Huawei with enough funds for further technical development. In 1994, a series of breakthroughs were made in voltage-fluctuation protection and optical transmission which greatly enhanced the attractiveness of its improved C&C08C system (with 10,000 lines capacity) in China's unstable network environment. At the same time Huawei began to use its own engineers to design key components such as core chip and PCB. Subsequently, in 1996, the flagship C&C08B system (also with 10,000 lines capacity) gained an advantage over foreign rivals with its high reliability in a high load environment. Huawei's C&C08 system also has perfect interconnection capabilities, with abundant narrowband and broadband user interfaces, and is designed for easy upgrading. It is much more user-friendly and convenient for local customers than the products of the MNCs. The software design work can support the additional new functions for future requirements of local customers. The C&C08 series product matched those of existing operators attached to MNCs and since 1995 has gradually become a substitute for many old foreign systems. In 2001, Huawei had 37.5% of the SPC market in China, 2.5% higher than the previous year. As to the in-house R&D output, Huawei has acquired 42 accredited patents relative to switching platform technology.

Huawei was inspired by its success in the SPC switch market but its desire to develop into a capable global competitor was not satisfied by this scenario. Huawei now began to extend its technological capabilities to the optical transmission, data communication and mobile communication sectors. Their efforts received quite positive feedback. For example, Huawei made a series of breakthroughs in designing and manufacturing some types of advanced SDH systems and had 40% of the optical transmission market in 2002 (CCID, 2003). These new products also perform competently when compared with foreign rivals, but offer the advantages of localized design, lower prices and competitive after-sales service.

In the mobile sector, GSM became the global mobile standard, just as CDMA emerged in the United States. Then, when China's carriers rolled out GSM networks nationwide, Huawei found itself shut out of the country's wealthier coastal provinces. All the major cities had already been covered. Along with domestic rival ZTE, Huawei was left with thin pickings in China's poorer hinterlandand before 2000, was fighting just to survive.

Huawei's catch-up in the wireless area clearly indicates how the gap between Huawei and global leaders has been decreased through its efforts with new generation mobile communication technologies, which took several years to come to fruition. In 2005, a year when new mobile network rollout slowed substantially, it supplied core infrastructure for nineteen new mobile networks – not far behind Nokia's 22 and Ericsson's 25, according to Information Telecoms and Media. In 2005, revenues from mobile network equipment accounted for nearly half of total revenues. However, Huawei's foreign contracts have been overwhelmingly in the developing world, where contracts tend to be much smaller compared with the leading global giants.

## Entry into globalized competition

Huawei is now also winning sizeable contracts in optical networks and next-generation networks (NGN) globally, and – significantly – has begun taking market share from Ericsson and Nokia in foreign wireless infrastructure. In 2006, Vodafone selected Huawei to build the radio access part of its UMTS/HSDPA Network in Spain. While there is no guarantee of future contracts, the agreement does admit Huawei to an exclusive club of vendors eligible to bid on Vodafone tenders. Telfort and Vodafone, as first-world carriers, provided welcome affirmation for a company that has invested heavily. And in April 2005, BT named Huawei as one of eight preferred vendors to supply equipment for the company's so-called 21st Century Network (21CN) project – a plan to integrate all its voice, data, and IP networks into a single, converged NGN by 2009. Competition was fierce, with over 50 vendors submitting bids. Huawei won contracts in two domains: it will supply multi-service access network (MSAN) equipment, which connects fibre, copper, and wireless lines to the network, along with co-winner Fujitsu, and optical transport equipment, which moves signals through fibre-optic lines, along with Ciena.

Huawei is not only competing with Cisco and Juniper in data communications equipment; it is also winning sizeable contracts in optical networks and NGNs and has even begun taking market share from global players like Ericsson and Nokia in new wireless infrastructure. With a third of its 18,000-strong R&D operation deployed in the third-generation (3G) and mobile sectors, Huawei has capabilities in all three 3G standards, plus China's home-grown 3G standard, putting it in a strong position it to win big 3G contracts at home. Huawei is also keeping up with competition in newer technologies like high-speed downlink packet access (HSDPA) and WiMAX, giving it a good chance of making inroads in developed markets in the next round of network building. Huawei has in fact supplied eighteen commercial WCDMA networks to date (Wideband CDMA, gibberish to most people, comes down to speedier cellular transmission, enabling, for example, phone TV). Given the extent of WCDMA (and GSM) coverage in Europe, there is little room for Huawei to get in and sell. In July 2006, eMobile, a mobile operator in Japan, selected Huawei as a key 3G equipment supplier for the rollout of its new UMTS and HSDPA network, which is Japan's first IP-based HSDPA Radio Access Network. Company and country alike are transforming the global competitive landscape with the rock-bottom prices their cheap, seemingly inexhaustible talent pools make possible.

## Global ambitions and upgrading

In 2001, Huawei decided to look abroad in search of green field markets, paying its way with proceeds from the sale that year of its telecom power systems unit to Emerson for $750 million. As the government was encouraging hi-tech firms to export, the company also established easy credit arrangements, lining up a $600 million credit facility with the Export-Import Bank of China and the China Development Bank. Its portfolio of end-to-end solutions also appealed because, as one industry report notes, developing country operators tend to lack expertise and seek out turnkey solutions. Huawei arrived as a primary global contender in 2005, when international contract sales of $4.75

billion outpaced domestic sales, accounting for 58% of 2005's $8.2 billion revenue (Red Herring, 2006).

With the foundations built and experience already accumulated, Huawei improved through painful internal restructuring that shook up the basic organizational structure of the firm, resulting in reformed product lines and client lines, and an enhanced role for the marketing department. All these were initially triggered by Huawei's desire to become a qualified supplier of British Telecom. Further, Huawei took a drastically different approach to building its external image as a global high-tech company through improving the transparency of the company, enhancing advertisements, and redesigning its logo. The changes of this period were essential to the transformation of Huawei from a local producer to a global giant.

### Painful restructuring

Huawei's painful restructuring can be characterized as a client-pull process, originating in Huawei's desire to develop into a world-level supplier by becoming one of the main suppliers of world-level service providers. British Telecom, one of the largest telecom service providers in the world, happened to be Huawei's first target. In order to become a supplier of British Telecom, Huawei had to obtain BT's supplier certification through a lengthy process that examined twelve different aspects of the company, including marketing, supply, human resources, finance and sales. At the time Huawei, was confident about BT's examination as it had implemented integrated product development (IPD) in 1998 and integrated supply chain (ISC) in 2000. Moreover, consultants from IBM had helped Huawei to improve in other respects. In November 2003, British Telecom's certification team arrived at Huawei for a four-day examination. The evaluation result showed that Huawei obtained high scores on the "hardware" of basic infrastructure, but not "software," such as business processing ability. Huawei realized that to bridge the gap between their performance and BT's expectation, the company had to improve its competitiveness through internal restructuring, triggering a series of structural reforms (Wu & Yi, 2006).

A series of internal changes thus commenced. First, Huawei realized that to become the strategic partner of global level service providers, such as BT, it needed to have an end-to-end team for each customer. It therefore set up one-to-one global teams for targeted large global providers, usually led by chief executive officers in the respective countries. In addition, Huawei standardized its working language, from R&D, marketing, salesand supply chain, to working languagesand product explanation notes, to enable dialogue with its clients in terms that were understood in the industry. The traditional approach utilized by Huawei in domestic markets, deploying multiple sales personnel to build a relationship with clients, does not really work with international clients, who are more concerned with gaining new profitable business.

Second, Huawei adjusted its product lines to fit the development of the global telecom industry. On the one hand, subsectors, such as optical fibre networks, access equipment and data communication, were consolidated into one comprehensive network solution unit. On the other hand, second and third generation mobile communication equipment and wireless access equipment were merged into one mobile solution unit. Huawei separated the business network into an independent unit for development that included business and software products. The unit has developed applied products such as IPTV and ICT and had about 3,000 employees in 2006.

Third, to match its global expansion needs, Huawei further restructured its regional division. The original divisions of marketing and sales departments, domestic and oversea markets, were regrouped into nine regions, and China became just one of the regions. To improve reaction speeds in the oversea markets, every region has a regional headquarters. Since 2005, little difference has existed between the domestic and oversea markets. Through the restructuring, Huawei has achieved an organization structure very similar to IBM's multi-dimensional matrix, with four main dimensions: product lines, client lines, support platforms and regional divisions. In addition to the internal restructuring, Huawei, with its low-profile policy, transformed its external image. Since the Cisco lawsuit, Huawei has realized that retaining its mysterious image will only create misunderstanding and barriers to its globalizing efforts. Thus, in order to let the media and clients know about the real Huawei, it started image-building on a large scale, actively attending local exhibitions and discussion forums and communicating closely with various influential organizations. For instance, in March 2005, when the largest global IT exhibition CeBIT was held in Hanover, Huawei organized the second industrial analysts' conference in Hamburg and presented its view of the development trend of the industry and laid out its product lines, with detailed marketing and financial data, even though it was not a public company. Moreover, it ramped up its advertising in the overseas markets; full pages of Huawei's commercial ads could be found in *The Economist, Business Week, Total Telecom,* and *IT Week*. In 2006, the logo was redesigned: the symbol of Huawei was changed from fifteen rays to eight beautiful flower petals, a further indication of Huawei's efforts to merge with main-stream culture, thus improving its image as a global leader.

The strategic restructuring and image rebuilding were essential to Huawei's transformation into a major global player. In April 2005, as we have seen, Huawei, along with eight other global giants such as Cisco, Siemens, and Lucent, became BT's priority suppliers for CNC, a project with investment capital of £10–19 billion in the next five years. Furthermore, Cisco and Huawei were the only two producers that would supply equipment in two of the five sub-sectors, all other producers only supplying in one sub-sector. *The Economist* commented that the rise of Huawei may be the disaster of other global multinationals (Wu & Yi, 2006).

### Future strength

Huawei's hypermodern headquarters outside Shenzhen, a city across the border from Hong Kong, sprawls across 320 acres of neatly trimmed lawns and tropical foliage. It is built to impress: elegant buildings, a cavernous exhibition hall, a network command centre sitting atop an enormous server farm, resembling a Hollywood vision of NORAD's Cheyenne Mountain facility. The heart of the operation is the tall, forbidding R&D building, dubbed "The Tower of Ten Thousand Engineers" by some industry insiders. It is actually home to about half that number, the company says, but it is almost home in a literal sense – many engineers keep bedrolls handy for power naps between marathon work sessions.

Huawei's R&D investment is comparable to that of other major multinational corporations in the telecom-equipment industry (Fan, 2006), whereas the R&D staff as a percentage of its workforce (48%) is higher than the global average.

Of Huawei's 37,000 employees spread across China and 40 other countries, 18,000 were in R&D in 2006. Huawei's R&D expenditure is dwarfed by competitors like Ericsson ($2.95 billion in 2004) or Nokia

($4.65 billion) – but R&D dollars go much further in China and in China Huawei is a huge spender: 14% of revenues in 2004 and 2005 went to R&D, an unheard of ratio, and it has not spent less than 10% since 1993. Huawei now leads China in total number of patents filed, with over 8,000, according to the State Intellectual Property Office. In the first half of 2005 alone, it filed 1,231 patents; about 800 have been filed to date in the US and Europe (Huawei website). As it courts first-tier operators, Huawei has had to pull back the curtains, at least for its potential customers, and its high-profile wins have certainly helped burnish its image.

## Lenovo

On 1 May 2005, Lenovo Group of China and IBM announced the acquisition of IBM's Personal Computing Division by Lenovo, creating a new international IT giant and the third largest personal computing firm in the world. Under the terms of the transaction, Lenovo had to pay IBM US$1.25 billion, comprising approximately US$650 million in cash and US$600 million in Lenovo Group shares, which made up 18.5% (IBM's proportion of total shares in Lenovo Group). The acquisition of IBM's PC business is a historic event for Chinese ICT companies: a breakthrough for Chinese companies into the global market and the possible beginning of a new era of the acquisition of world-famous brands by aggressive Chinese companies.

### Domestic Success

In 1984, eleven computer scientists from the Chinese Academy of Sciences in Beijing, with RMB200,000 (US$25,000) in seed money and the determination to turn their research into successful products, set up shop in a loaned space – a small, one-story bungalow in Beijing. The company they founded, Legend, opened a new era of consumer PCs in China. It first introduced PCs to households, then promoted PC usage in China by establishing nationwide retail networks. It also developed the Chinese Character Card that translated English operating software into Chinese characters. At first, it became a distributor for AST from the US, and later for HP and other foreign branded PCs.

In the 1980s, the China's government decided to develop China's PC industry as a priority and as part of its broader, long-term goal of achieving self-reliance in the technological sectors. Legend began to manufacture PCs, selling them under its own brand name in mainland China and establishing a strong distribution channel for Legend and imported brands. By 1994, Legend was trading on the Hong Kong Stock Exchange; four years later, it produced its one-millionth personal computer. In 1999, Legend became the first Chinese PC manufacturer to be the top seller (by units) in the Asia-Pacific region (excluding Japan). In 1997 it overtook both IBM and Compaq as the leading PC supplier in China, and since then has remained in first place and expanded its share to almost 30% of the Chinese market (see Table 5.2). Such extreme adaptation to a particular domestic market, however, may be a liability if the firm wants to expand to new markets, especially those outside its home market (Xie & White, 2004).

*Table 5.2*   Market shares of top three PC manufacturers in China (%)

| Rank | 1996 | 1997 | 1998 | 2002 |
|------|------|------|------|------|
| 1 | COMPAQ (9.2) | Lenovo (10.7) | Lenovo (21.5) | Lenovo (27.3) |
| 2 | IBM (6.9) | IBM (7.5) | IBM (6.2) | IBM (9.0) |
| 3 | Lenovo (6.9) | COMPAQ (6.7) | Founder (5.9) | Founder (5.0) |

*Sources*: Lu (2000), IDC (2002).

Legend entered the mobile handset and IT management consultancy businesses in 2002. In 2003, it changed its brand name to Lenovo, taking the "Le" from Legend, a nod to its heritage, and adding "novo", the Latin word for "new", to reflect the spirit of innovation at the core of the company.

In 2003, Lenovo introduced a self-developed collaborative application technology, which heralds the important role Lenovo is going to play in the 3C era (computer, communications and consumer electronics). These and other market-leading personal computing products catapulted Lenovo to a leadership position in China for eight consecutive years with over 25% market share in 2004.

The competitive advantages of Lenovo the home PC market in China, Lenovo wanted to introduce a new generation of products by building manufacturing capacity benefiting from greater economies of scale and by taking advantage of component cost reductions faster than its competitors. At the same time, Lenovo established strong partnerships with Intel, Microsoft, IBM, HP and Texas Instruments, and the disciplined execution of the channel policy created a very strong and loyal channel. Lenovo's case shows that an initial set of resources and capabilities can support the development of additional complementary ones; it also demonstrates the evolutionary and path-dependent nature of capability development.

### New Lenovo at the global stage

With Lenovo's landmark acquisition of IBM's PC division in May 2005, the new Lenovo has become a leader in the global PC market, with approximately US$13 billion in annual revenue and products serving enterprises and consumers the world over. To promote its brand reputation, Lenovo became a worldwide partner of the International Olympic Committee in 2004. The company provided computing technology equipment for the 2006 Turin Olympic Winter Games and the 2008 Beijing Olympic Summer Games.

### Strategic fit between complementary organizations

By acquiring IBM's PC division and brand using rights, Lenovo has achieved a near-perfect fit between these two complementary organizations in terms of brand recognition, market expertise and core resources. As a premium global PC brand, the expertise of IBM in business markets, especially in Notebook products, will be of great benefit to Lenovo. Under the agreement, IBM promised to help the new Lenovo to expand their marketing and sales channel; help them to improve their research and development capability and consolidate well in terms of corporate culture and management. IBM had received fixed orders (worth US$1 billion annually) from the US government and other official organizations, making up 10% of its PC division, but it is difficult for Lenovo to keep these government customers. The number of American enterprise customers will also be reduced while new Lenovo becomes more established in the four key emerging countries: China, India, Brazil, Russia.

We can conclude that the following are key l factors for the success of the new Lenovo in global operations:

- Create strong image of quality and innovation outside China
- Gain market share by building more economies of scale and purchasing power
- Become the market leader in emerging regions

- Successfully enter the consumer market in NA (North America), EMEA (Europe Middle East and Africa)
- Protect and continue to develop successful IBM brands
- Merge two cultures into a single company

Lenovo strives to be a new world company that makes the world's best-engineered PCs for its customers. They try to operate as a company uninhibited by walls or organizational structures using global sourcing to harness the power of innovation across its worldwide team. It designs innovative and exciting products and services to meet customers' needs. Lenovo's mobile phone division is one of its fastest growing businesses, according to the company. Mostly known for its PCs, Lenovo now also claims 7% of the Chinese market – the world's largest cellular market – after Nokia, Motorola and Samsung.

## TCL

TCL is a leading multi-electronics company. It was founded in 1980 as a Guangdong-based cassette manufacturer, and by 1986 had become the number one telephone producer in China. In 1992, TCL entered the TV industry, at first as a distributor – it sold colour televisions produced by its Hong Kong based joint venture partner, under TCL's King brand. In 1996,it moved into production, forming a joint venture with a Hong Kong manufacturer to produce televisions in Shenzhen. It then started to expand its production capacity and presence in many Chinese cities, producing 16 million sets a year and covering the entire Chinese market. In 2006, TCL's annual television sales in China increased to 14 million sets, maintaining its number one position (TCL website).

TCL's international expansion began in 1997, when it started to export CRT television sets first to the United States and then to Southeast Asia. In 1999, it took over the Luk factory in Vietnam with the intention of fulfilling local demand and further expanding the Southeast Asian market. By 2006, TCL held 22% of Vietnam's CRT TV market, ranking second behind Samsung Electronics of Korea.

Global prominence came in January 2004, when TCL and Thomson signed an agreement to create TTE, a joint venture that combined the CRT TV assets of each. TCL dominated the joint venture, with 38% shares, with Thomson holding 30%. Five regional business centers

(RBCs) – China, Europe, North America, Strategic Original Equipment Manufacturer OEM) and EM (Emerging Markets) – were established to manage the sales and marketing function of TTE CRT TV products globally. Each RBC was responsible for a specific market, with a different market focus and brand.

To expand manufacturing-based activity to overseas countries, TCL adopted two kinds of entry route: mergers and acquisitions (M&A) and outsourcing. TTEV was acquired from Luk Industrial; TTET, TTEP and TTEM were obtained from Thomson; factories in Indonesia, the Philippines and India are all CMS plants. Under the agreement, TTE owns 10 manufacturing plants worldwide, six in China and one in each of Vietnam, Thailand, Poland and Mexico. The latter three factories were previously owned by Thomson. As a result, TTE is capable of producing 23 million TV sets each year, the biggest capacity in the world. In 2006, TCL's CRT TV overseas sales reached 9 million sets, while domestic sales were 8.85 million. During 2004–2006 apart from some procurement adjustments, overseas factories and supply chains operated almost the same as before M&A. Inevitably, TTE has been affected by Thomson's huge losses. In October 2006, TCL Group decided to exit the European TV market, hoping to staunch losses in the region. The decision cost it 45 million euros in restructuring charges. Pulling out of Europe was a big move for the company, and an indicator of how tough it is for Chinese brands to turn around the ailing assets of Western companies. With global sales of $5.8 billion in 2007, and serving more than 100 million consumers worldwide, TCL Corporation comprises four business units – Multimedia, Communications, Home Appliances and Techne Electronics. It also has two affiliated business networks: Real Estate & Investment and Logistics & Services. TCL is one of the world's leading producers of flat panel TVs, DVD players, air conditioners, and GSM CDMA mobile phones. TCL's production and sales network has spread to dozens of countries and regions throughout the world. The company has seven R&D centres, seventeen manufacturing facilities, 40,000 sales locations and centralized management (product design and manufacturing, logistics supply, quality assurance, and product innovation and support). TCL has also taken advantage of its joint venture with Alcatel to substantially increase its exports of handsets. These rose sevenfold in the year to August 2005, to 494,716 units. TCL is also planning to produce 3G handsets in China using Philips. It plans to reduce overseas employees to cut costs.

## Spreadtrum: semiconductor star

In the brain-intensive, fiercely competitive, rapid growth environment of integrated circuit (IC) design, intellectual property (IP)-related legal issues have a critical impact on the market discipline of fair competition and on the willingness of global investors. Established in 2001, Spreadtrum is a semiconductor design company based in Shanghai that develops and markets baseband processor solutions for the 2G, 2.5G, 3G and B3G wireless communications markets. The company's first project was a baseband chip for 2.5G GPRS handsets. Success came in 2002 when it developed its first GPRS chip. Later, in April and May 2003, other companies started taking notice of Spreadtrum's 2.5G chip and orders began to flow in from local handset manufacturers. By developing the mainstream GSM/GPRS chip, Spreadtrum survived. It now employs 800 design engineers, 700 of whom are software engineers.

Spreadtrum has achieved a critical breakthrough in Chinese standard core technologies. This is surely a positive development. On 23 October 2007, Spreadtrum Communications (NASDAQ. SPRD) announced that ZTE's Shanghai R&D centre had successfully implemented TD-MBMS service based on its TD-SCDMA/GSM/GPRS dual-radio chip solution. TD-MBMS is a mobile multimedia service application solution deployed on TD-SCDMA networks that supports uni-cast and multicast streams of media like TV programmes on mobile handsets. TD-SCDMA is a 3G standard independently developed by China. Spreadtrum successfully acquired US-based Radio Frequency (RF) IC design company Quorum Systems Inc. to perfect its product portfolio. Not long afterwards, China Netcom announced at the commercial release celebration of its Audio Video Coding Standard Interactive based IPTV in Dalian, that its set top boxes (STBs) that adopt the SV6111 AVS chip solution provided by Spreadtrum had been approved without a hitch. AVS is a 2G information source coding standard also independently developed by China.

China Mobile has, however, postponed its planned bidding and procurement of TD-SCDMA handsets, and AVS_IPTV has not been widely deployed in China – it will be a long time before Spreadtrum can benefit from the Chinese standard. Much of the company's revenue comes from GSM/GPRS handset baseband chips that currently dominate the international market. It also follows the other two mainstream 2G information source coding standards, H.264 and MPEG4, closely, and has listed both as priorities on its R&D agenda over the next two years.

Spreadtrum was founded in 2001 by Wu Ping, Chen Datong and two colleagues, all of whom had returned from California's infamous Silicon Valley. They started making baseband chips for WCDMA handsets, telling investors that WCDMA was the dominant 3G standard.

The company's first project was a baseband chip for 2.5G GPRS handsets. Success came in 2002 when it developed its first GPRS chip. Later, in April and May 2003, other companies started to notice Spreadtrum's 2.5G chip and orders began to flow in from local handset manufacturers. By developing the mainstream GSM/GPRS chip, Spreadtrum survived in the market.

But the company soon came to a difficult choice regarding 3G. Whether it should develop mainstream WCDMA chips or start work on domestic TD-SCDMA chips became a major issue. After careful consideration, Spreadtrum chose to develop TD-SCDMA chips first. More appealing was the fact that only a few Chinese companies were developing TD-SCDMA chips. What happened next turned out exactly as the company had expected: Spreadtrum became the first global IC designer to develop baseband chips for TD-SCDMA handsets. Spreadtrum was in fact keenly aware of major changes taking place in the global technology market. Having become one of the world's most important markets, China started to demand a say in the establishment of home-grown international technology standards, while also developing standards of its own. This is what the Chinese government hopes to see and it offers a reassuring level of encouragement for technology companies like Spreadtrum that appear able to make this important leap (Merritt, 2008).

Spreadtrum has thus followed the government's lead in choosing to develop home-made standards. It has done so thus far with the TD-SCDMA and AVS standards. As an information source coding system, AVS can be widely applied in IPTV, digital TV and handset TV streaming. If it can be rapidly and widely appled, it is likely to become the second Chinese standard, after TD-SCDMA. Consequently, Spreadtrum, as promoter, will have a larger market share. Spreadtrum is, as a result, oscillating between Chinese and international standards. The company is currently focused on TD-SCDMA chips and is targeting the WCDMA chip market which will shortly be appearing in China.

Before going public at the end of June 2007, Spreadtrum survived a trying ordeal. Because the chip industry has a high technology threshold and requires a large investment to ensure successful development, the company had been thirsty for funds from the day it was established, and it had to launch several fundraising campaigns in order to address this problem. It collected over US$60 million from between twenty and thirty venture capitals before going public. The company's most difficult period came during its second year of operations. From June 2002, the company was short of funds and had to raise a considerable amount of cash. But the Silicon Valley slump that began in 2000 put a stop to a great deal of venture capital, especially that flowing to countries like China. In spite of Spreadtrum having developed its own 2.5G baseband chip and showcased it to investors, it was still difficult to find interested parties. To sustain R&D, the company lowered wages, up to 50% for top management and 30% for middle management. It even toyed with scrapping wages entirely. Fortunately, it successfully raised enough funds to survive in October 2002. After Spreadtrum's entrance into the TD-SCDMA market, the senior management of an international chip giant declared its interest in buying the Chinese company.

Of its eight-person board, only Wu Ping and Chen Datong come from the Spreadtrum management. Fortunately, the board has so far been very supportive of and satisfied with the management and has refrained from interfering with the development of the company. But this does not mean capital and management will be conflict free. To ensure that the company can further expand along the road they have defined, both Wu and Chen need to play a more sophisticated balancing act.

In August, 2007, Spreadtrum showcased its MocorTM platform which, based on the multi-mode single-chip solution of the company, could provide clients with turnkey solutions including communications software, application software, reference designs, development boards, development tools and technical support. The forum attracted many handset vendors and chip vendors as well as software and application service providers.

Spreadtrum has indicated that in future it will be more focused on providing core technology platforms for its partners, rather than engaging in developing application layers. This means the company is bidding farewell to its past. Previously, what it did was no different from MTK, and both companies provided clients with turnkey services – local handset manufacturers only needed to provide outside casing for their handsets. It was because of this that MTK and Spreadtrum defeated TI and other international chip giants in the local market and gained the upper hand. In 2006, Spreadtrum took 10% of the local 2G/2.5G handset chip market, second only to MTK and TI. At that time, local handset manufacturers lacked R&D abilities and chipmakers were forced to shoulder more R&D responsibilities.

But the 3G era is likely to require something completely different. As more and more operators dominate the industrial chain with handset customization, manufacturers need increasingly to integrate R&D and resources. Only those that can swiftly respond to operator requirements have a good chance of survival. Chipmakers that do not maintain direct contact with operators will never be able to satisfy application demands as required. Chipmakers then need to focus on core platforms if they are to succeed in the future. Spreadtrum has realized this and on 27 May 2007, in conjunction with Wingtech Group, the largest domestic handset designer in China, it began to establish a 3G-handset industry base in Zhejiang province. Huawei is reportedly a key client of the base.

In August 2007, Spreadtrum signed a strategic partnership with ZTE. Notably, the company concluded a cooperation agreement with ZTE's TD-SCDMA system rather than its handset department. This is an important step for Spreadtrum in implementing its platform-oriented strategy. With a heavyweight partner like ZTE, Spreadtrum will be freed from application-layer technologies. Instead, it will be able to concentrate on a chip platform business that can deliver more value.

Spreadtrum's financial report indicates that handset baseband solutions have contributed an increasing amount to revenue, rising from 7% to 85% in the 2nd quarter of 2007. In the meantime, the share of its turnkey business dropped from 93% in the second quarter of 2005 to 15% in the second quarter of 2007. The platform strategy has produced instant results and the gross margin has jumped from an initial 19.2% to 45.5% (Ji, 2007).

After Spreadtrum secured a firm foothold, many venture capitals that missed their chance to invest in the company started to look for similar tech ventures to dump their money into. Spreadtrum is the only baseband chip maker in the world to be listed in US in the past decade.

In November 2007, Spreadtrum acquired Quorum Systems Inc., a fabless semiconductor company that specializes in the design of CMOS radio frequency transceivers. Quorum's RF technology, combined with its strengths in complete baseband and software solutions, will allow Spreadtrum to strengthen its position in the competitive mobile wireless communications market, from 2G to 3G, from RF to baseband, from physical layer software to protocol and applications (LaPedus, 2007).

Though the Chinese semiconductor design industry has undergone tremendous growth, it remains quite small compared with the rest of the world. Chinese standards, government support and services targeted at the local market are the most powerful weapons in the fight against international competitors. Domestic companies have been forced to realize that success required them to focus on some other areas. When tracking down overseas capital for growth, they should also be aware of the risk of being taken over, so a fine balance is required. Unfortunately, few companies manage to achieve this. In a sense, Spreadtrum and Vimicro stand as excellent examples.

## SINA.com

The quick penetration of the Internet in China has provided great opportunities for the expansion of Internet portals like SINA. Despite their early advantage and superior technology, foreign.-based portals have failed to challenge strong local portals under China's specific cultural and institutional environment.

SINA Corporation was founded in March 1999 through the merger of Beijing SINA Information Technology and California-based SINANET.com. In April 2000, the company completed its initial public offering and was listed on the NASDAQ market which maybe the biggest milestone of its growth. Incorporated in the Cayman Islands, SINA has headquarters in Shanghai, offices in seven cities and a network of four websites around the world. The primary focus of its operations is undoubtedly in China, Where its business operations are conducted primarily through significant wholly-owned subsidiaries, including Sina.com Technology (China), Beijing New Media Information Technology, Fayco Network Technology Development (Shenzhen), and Beijing SINA Internet Technology Service.

SINA has completed a number of important acquisitions to expand the business over the past few years, including the acquisition of Memestar in 2003, Crillion Corporation in 2004 and Davidhill Capital in 2004. From 1999 to 2001, SINA's growth was mainly driven by the online advertising business, which generated the majority of the total revenues. SINA began offering mobile value-added services (MVAS) under arrangements with third-party operators in the PRC in late 2001 and have up until 2004 experienced significant growth in MVAS revenues.

### Business overview

Learned from the downturn of internet bubble in Western countries, the Chinese internet companies like SINA try to have the well-diversified revenues. Before 2004, SINA was an Internet portal providing comprehensive services such as Web searching, e-mail, news, business directory, entertainment, weather forecast, etc. Now SINA is positioned as an online media company and value-added information service provider in the People's Republic of China and the global Chinese communities. With a branded network of localized web sites targeting Greater China and overseas Chinese, the Company provides services through five major business lines including SINA.com, SINA Mobile (MVAS), SINA Community, SINA.net (search and enterprise services) and SINA E-Commerce (online shopping). Together these business lines provide an array of services including region-specific online portals, MVAS, search and directory, interest-based and community-building channels, free and premium email, blog services, audio and video streaming, game community services, classified listings, fee-based services, e-commerce and enterprise e-solutions. The company generates the majority of its revenues from online advertising and MVAS offerings, and, to a lesser extent, from search and other fee-based services.

SINA offers distinct and targeted content on each of its region-specific web sites, with a range of complementary offerings designed to broaden its user base and increase user traffic. The company aims to become the media platform of choice for internet users to research and retrieve information and for businesses to market and promote their products. SINA's complementary offerings are all centered on its core content business and are intended to enhance the attractiveness of its portal business and strengthen its reach in the community.

As the leader in internet word of China, to build an ecosystem around the internet portal is critical to the success of SINA. In 2007, SINA continued to focus on strengthening its multimedia and community-based product offerings. One new area of focus has been integrating user generated contents, such as blog into traditional website verticals. In addition, upgrades to email and instant messages were launched to strengthen the communication aspect of SINA Community product offerings to adhere the customers.

Actually, SINA has built up several interactive platforms including SINA Music and SINA Game. Through these integrated platforms, internet users may not only obtain information and updates but also interactively communicate with other community members with similar interests. In the video sphere, the SINA continued to invest in the acquisition of quality contents and optimization of content distribution infrastructure in an effort to transform SINA from a text-based media platform to a multimedia and community-based media platform. In 2007, SINA also expanded its strategic relationships into various areas including content, service and distribution to build the business ecosystem. In May 2007, the Company formed strategic alliance with China Telecom, one of the largest telecom operators, to provide a co-branded video sharing platform. With this partnership, SINA is able to offer a scalable solution for video sharing with the support of the largest telecommunication network operator in China. In June 2007, SINA entered into a partnership agreement with Google, whereby the two parties agreed to cooperate on search, advertising and branding.

To prepare for the 2008 Beijing Olympics, SINA has taken several initiatives to enhance its leadership in the online media, particular in the area of sports. In 2007, the Company obtained a series of new media rights to broadcast some of the most popular sporting events in China, many of which are on an exclusive basis, such as matches from the English Premier League and the European Championship. In addition, SINA launched an integrated marketing campaign named "My 2008: The World Opens Its Eyes." The year-long campaign leading up to the 2008 Beijing Olympics is designed to encourage internet users to share their views, thoughts and feelings about the 2008 Beijing Olympics and its impact on China and the Chinese people via SINA Blog, SINA Podcast or SINA Album. The Olympic Channel (http://2008.sina.com.cn/en) under SINA English offers the latest news, videos, photos, facts and figures of the Beijing Olympic Games with insights into China, its people and culture. Leveraging its leadership in sports coverage and local expertise, SINA's seasoned editorial team has tracked the up-to-date Olympic news, provide a wide range of hotspot information of the 29th Olympic Games and provided special commentaries and interesting discussions on the various aspects of the Olympics, such as the stories behind the Olympic emblem, mascot and torch as well as introduction to the host cities around China (Sina, 2009).

## Market opportunities

SINA is primarily focused on but not limited to the Chinese market. The success of its business is linked to the size and vitality of China's economy and global Chinese community. In a preliminary study published by the Chinese National Bureau of Statistics, China's gross domestic product (GDP) reached $3.2 trillion in 2007, representing an 11.4% year-on-year growth rate. The latest survey by China Internet Network Information Centre (CNNIC) shows that internet users in China have grown 53.3% from 2006 to 210 million as of the end of 2007. Actually, the large user base makes China an attractive market for the SINA to expand its internet product and service offerings and to grow its revenue streams. According to the survey by CNNIC, 78% of the users in China have access to the internet via broadband (CNNIC, 2007). The widespread adoption of broadband creates opportunities for the online industry, particularly in the areas of audio and video-based products and services, such as lucrative media and video advertising. With the Chinese government issuing 3G wireless licenses at the beginning of 2009, the issuing of multiple 3G licenses would level the playing field among the telecom operators, improve the performance of internet access via mobile phones and significantly broaden the reach of the internet in a broader scope.

SINA is also serving as a one-stop-shopping hub for various franchise chains. Based on the allied franchise systems, the portals may create value-added services to the targeted customers. For example, the alliance with Yafei Auto Chain enables Sina.com to create a new car leasing business as a network organization the franchise system's may help web portals plan the network solutions to their franchise customers.

### SINA.com online

SINA is also an online brand advertising property in China. SINA employs a multi-pronged sales strategy that targets both short-term revenue opportunities such as banner advertising campaigns and longer-term, higher value contracts that include integrated marketing packages. From the website of SINA, we can find that the company's advertising product offerings consist of banner, button, text-link advertisements that appear on pages within the SINA network, channel and promotional sponsorships, and advertising campaign design and management services. Regional companies consist of medium to large companies that are focused on specific geographic and demographic markets, such as Chinese Americans or Taiwanese, and smaller companies whose markets are within a local territory, such as Beijing or Hong Kong. A partial list of advertising clients includes: China Mobile, Intel, Lenovo, Meng Niu Dairy, Microsoft, Nike, Samsung and Toyota. By the end of 2007, SINA had approximately 740 advertisers worldwide. Advertiser customers from the automobile, real estate and information technology industris contributed over half of the total online advertising dollars in 2007 (Sina Annual Report, 2008).

Now, the SINA's portal network consists of four destination websites dedicated to its users across the globe: mainland China (www.sina.com.cn), Taiwan (www.sina.com.tw), Hong Kong www.sina.com.hk), and overseas Chinese in North America (www.sina.com). Each destination site consists of Chinese-language news and content organized into interest-based channels. The sites offer extensive community and communication services and sophisticated web navigation capability through SINA search and directory services.

SINA.com offers a variety of free interest-based channels that provide region-focused format and content. The most popular channel is *SINA News*. SINA News aggregates feeds from news providers, bringing together content from media companies such as China News, Agence France-Presse (AFP), Associated Press, Reuters, Getty Images, China Daily, Nanfang Daily Group, Beijing News, Xinhua Net and Xinhua News Agency. Through SINA News, users have easy access to breaking news coverage from multiple sources and points of view.

Launched in 2005, SINA Blog has quickly become a popular platform for Chinese bloggers to read and publish original writings. SINA Mobile, SINA's MVAS, launched in April 2002, allows users to receive news and information, download ring tones and pictures, and participate in dating and friendship communities. Users can order these services through the SINA website or through their mobile phones on a monthly subscription, or pay on a per message basis. SINA's competitive advantage in MVAS comes from its online and offline marketing channels as well as from its large user numbers and unique online content brand.

At the offline area, SINA also has a large local sales team that covers the majority of the provinces and municipalities in China as well as a significant presence in local TV, radio and print advertising. SINA has established content partnerships with certain international record label companies to provide image and music downloads. SINA Mobile provides MVAS mainly through operator platforms, including the Monternet platform of China Mobile and the UNI-Info platform of China Unicom. SINA also works closely with provincial-level operators to jointly promote its MVAS offerings. SINA's MVAS can be categorized into three main categories: news and information, community, and multimedia downloads. SINA provides its MVAS mainly through *SINA SMS*. As many mobile phones are able to display and send text in Chinese, SINA has developed a suite of short messaging services that includes user-customized information subscription, personal greetings, customized mobile phone screen decoration, personalized ring tones and mobile games.

### Strategic relationships

SINA has developed strategic relationships with a range of content, service, application and distribution partners in order to serve users more effectively and to extend its brand and services to a broader audience.

### Content partnerships

The goal of SINA's content partnerships is to provide its users with a large offering of Chinese-language content. SINA contracts with content partners to display their content on one or more of its websites free of charge or in exchange for a share of revenue, a licensing fee, and access to SINA-generated content, or a combination of these arrangements.

### Application and service partnerships

The goal of SINA's application and service partnerships is to ensure that its users have access to user-friendly, reliable and measurable communication and search tools. Because many of the Company's prospective partners have traditionally focused on non-Chinese speaking markets, SINA's internal engineering and development teams often work closely with them to localize their solutions for the Chinese-language market.

### Technology infrastructure

SINA's basic operating infrastructure is designed to deliver hundreds of millions of page views per day to its huge users, allowing them to access its products and services regardless of their geographical location. The Company's web pages are generated, served and cached by servers hosted at various co-location web hosting sites in China, the U.S., Taiwan and Hong Kong.

On the mobile side, the Company is actively competing with other service providers. As SINA continues to broaden its range of product offerings, it expects increasing competition from these established players and possibly less well-known players in the coming years. Many of these competitors have strong financial resources and brand recognition in their respective niche sectors. In addition, certain companies, especially early-stage venture-backed start-ups, may be willing to compete for market share at the expense of generating revenues which may make the market more turbulent then.

Other online content/services companies compete with SINA for user traffic, advertising revenue, e-commerce transactions, MVAS and other fee-based services. Industry consolidation may occur as the market for the internet in China matures, which could result in increased competition. The company is also facing the competition from global internet companies such as Yahoo, Microsoft, eBay, Google and AOL. With the gradual opening of the telecommunications sector resulting from China's entry into the World Trade Organization, the company is facing an increasing number of international portals and internet companies to enter the Chinese online media industry and these companies may have longer operating histories. Interestingly, SINA is also competing for advertisers with traditional media companies, such as well-established newspapers, television networks and radio stations that have a longer history and greater acceptance among traditional advertisers. In addition, providers of Chinese language internet tools and services may be acquired by, receive investments from, or enter into other commercial relationships with large, well-established and well-financed internet, media or other companies (SINA website).

SINA's future to compete successfully depends on many factors, including the quality of its content, the breadth, depth and ease of use of its services, its sales and marketing efforts, and the performance of its technology upgrading.

## Alibaba: e-commerce pioneer

Alibaba.com Limited, a member of the Alibaba Group, is the world's leading business-to-business (B2B) e-commerce company. It connects millions of buyers and suppliers from around the world every day through three marketplaces: an English-language marketplace (www.alibaba.com) for global importers and exporters, a Chinese-language marketplace (www.alibaba.com.cn) for domestic trade in China, and a Japanese-language marketplace (www.alibaba.co.jp) facilitating trade to and from Japan. Together, its marketplaces form a community of more than 32 million registered users from over 240 countries and regions.

Jack Ma, a former English teacher from the eastern Chinese city of Hangzhou, founded Alibaba.com with eighteen others in 1999 as a trading platform for smaller manufacturers to sell their wares. Since then Alibaba.com has grown into the premier online marketplace for small and medium-size companies around the world to identify potential trading partners and interact with each other to conduct business online. Alibaba.com became listed on the Hong Kong Stock Exchange on 6 November 2007 and is the flagship business of the Alibaba Group. With headquarters in Hong Kong, Alibaba.com has offices in over 30 cities across mainland China as well as in Taiwan, Hong Kong, Europe and the US. The company had around 6,000 full-time employees as of June 2008.

Among all the developing e-commerce businesses in China, Alibaba.com has received more attention than other firms. In July 2000, this company was featured by Forbes as its cover story and selected as the only company on the Forbes "Best of the Web: B2B" list founded in China (Doebele, 2000). Alibaba.com featured again on the same list in September 2001. The company's CEO, Jack Ma, was selected as one of the 100 Global Leaders for Tomorrow by the World Economic Forum, and was honored as a recipient of the Asian Business Association Business Leadership Award in 2001. In December 2001 it became the only B2B Webster with 1,000,000 registered business members from 202 countries. To date, Alibaba.com has become the world's largest online business-to-business (B2B) marketplace for global trade and plays host to China's leading domestic B2B trade communities. Alibaba.com offers an open ecosystem or small and medium-sized enterprises (SMEs), who can join with minimum requirements.

In selecting its business model and strategy, Alibaba.com has firmly oncentrated on B2B because it is not optimistic about the future of business-to-consumer (B2C) in China due to the barriers in unsolved ayment method, transportation and credit system (Zhang, 2000d). Alibaba.com also considers it impractical to conduct transaction online at this period of time in China. For online transactions, there are basically six levels: information exchange, negotiation, price bargaining, shipping, insurance, inspection and customs processing, and payment (Zhang, 2000). Alibaba.com ensures a reliable online payment process through a third-party payment website – Ali-pay. Its premium TrustPass® membership is another notable credit enhancing mechanism. Only members who have completed an authentication and verification procedure conducted by a third-party credit agency are granted TrustPass® qualification. TrustPass® serves to provide transparency regarding the identity and legitimacy of sellers and their potential trading partners with Alibaba.com. Information quality for TrustPass® membership is also guaranteed, thus increasing buyer confidence. More than 85% of buyers on Alibaba.com prefer to do business with members who have the TrustPass® qualification. In the transaction process Alibaba provides the credit mechanism through (1) TrustPass® member identity verification and (2) the third-party payment websites for the buyers and suppliers to make their transaction directly with one another.

## Value creation of Alibaba activities

The main activities of this e-market in each phase of transaction are outlined, and the complexity of controlling these activities to guarantee a secure and trustable transaction is evaluated.

### Personalized and customized services in Alibaba

In the information and the negotiation phases of the model, Alibaba offers personalized and customized services. Hundreds of product categories from 42 industries are presented in this market. Members are offered a utility called "ali-assistant" (or My Alibaba) to manage their product listing and internal websites. A wide array of trading functions are available for buyers and sellers to choose from, such as online auctions, online categories hosted in each member's site and real time negotiation conducted through a "Trade Manager". Through its three services, Ali-college, Ali-forum and TrustPass®, Alibaba users can be better serviced with less help from human agents. Ali-college is an online school maintained by Alibaba, and its purpose is to educate users on how to conduct business online. Ali-forum is an online discussion forum and also offers a blog hosting service. Online businessmen can also learn about products and business credits from the Ali-forum and TrustPass® services.

### Payment and delivery phases

A major concern in B2B e-markets is to carry out contract deals safely and reliably. In China, as in other nations, it is still possible that arrears and quality issues may occur in trading. Both parties are more worried about these unavoidable problems in the virtual market, and have reservations about security and trust in online trading. For example, if an on-line buyer is afraid of the quality of the products after the payment, then the quality inspection and refund should be warranted. In the B2B e-market, it needs a strategic partner's network formed by the bank system, the transportation entity and the quality inspection entity working together for a secure and reliable transaction process. To survive in the on-line business Alibaba established a network of business partners, including many banks and third parties. The third parties are mainly business credit rating companies and authentication agents.

Due to the complexity and cost of maintaining a logistic network, Alibaba does not help the buyer or seller to arrange the delivery of goods. However, Alibaba's payment process is intertwined with the delivery phase and involves multiple players from transportation and storage providers to customs agents and banks. Alibaba also focuses on controlling transaction risks present in the payment and delivery phase. By offering Ali-pay (Payment Bao), a third party payment service, Alibaba effectively controls these risks with lower operating cost. In Ali-pay, money is held by Ali-pay before buyers confirm receipt and quality of goods. The Ali-pay service can partially alleviate the problem of quality inspection and refund since this service supports product return and refund. When there are disputes, Ali-pay agents also contact logistics companies for information verification.

While e-businesses in China manage to survive and develop by employing a conservative business strategy, it is time for the Chinese government to step in actively in the development of e-commerce. In fact, e-commerce development strategy in China still needs government driving force at some time.

Although Alibaba has tried to maintain good relationships with the government, the government is generally not deeply involved in its business since it is a private entity under the regulation. In summary we can observe that Alibaba provides support in all transaction phases, increasing value either by controlling transactional risks, or by reducing transaction costs and enhancing efficiency (Zhao, 2008). Even though Alibaba has weaker support in the delivery phase, it cleverly allows participant involvement from both sides in fulfilling the contract. As a result, it satisfies customers and yet reduces costs. It is interesting that buyer and seller prefer to operate their own online transaction under a controlled transactional risk. Alibaba has exceeded the needs of users, so it is actually considered the most successful e-market platform in China. It is also noticeable that Alibaba's transactional process design requires less human involvement, increasing the capacity of its network and reducing operational cost.

For e-businesses such as Alibaba.com, it is imperative to pay attention to new legal issues emerging from e-commerce and to examine business strategies carefully in this large developing country. In addition to the explicit costs of hardware and software maintenance, technical support, facilities, education and communication line costs, it may be more important to consider and prepare for the implicit costs derived from legal risks and uncertainties, and to adjust and adopt appropriate business strategies accordingly (Hu & Wu, 2004).

## Summary

Knowledge of the drivers behind internationalization reveals not only the starting position of a company but also, importantly, the strategic direction they envisage for the future. There is varying emphasis on different aspects, depending on the company's strategic positioning within their specific area. As competition increases in their domestic market, greater numbers of Chinese companies will consider Western markets attractive for their products and services soon or later, the near future will see the targeting of Western countries and the subsequent internationalization of a number of these companies, which, regardless of their success or failure, will drastically change the existing conditions for Western companies (Söderman *et al.*, 2008).

If we consider the stage that China is reaching in its economic evolution and the role it is currently playing in the context of globalization, it is not strange for China to be eagerly involved in the battle to join the leading group in the globalized competitive battlefield. On the one hand, the country's spectacular development during the last 25 years, unparalleled in terms of speed and consequences for the world's economy in the rest area. On the other hand, it would be interesting to acquire deeper knowledge of the processes of outbound foreign direct investment undertaken by Chinese firms and the extent of the threat or opportunity that Chinese multinationals present in the new global scenario.

The gradual globalization of some China's leading ICT firms can be viewed as an orderly process from domestic operation, through exports and foreign direct investment to fully-fledged multinationals. The sequence of market entry matters much more for latecomers than for well-known MNCs due to latecomers' inexperience in international business, lack of established reputation and prejudices against the latecomer's country as a backward economy with doubtful capacity for innovation. The experience gives us an opportunity to theorize about how appropriate market entry can help to train latecomers in emerging countries. There are cost considerations affecting this process. The multinational competitors are stretching their research dollars, too, and establishing R&D facilities in China – and as competition for talent hots up, local firms will inevitably find it costlier to keep their own engineers in the face of the competing attraction of MNCs.

The Chinese national champions have a huge home base market that gives them a chance to continue honing their skills for future forays into the overseas battlefield. Through global expansion, China's pioneering firms have been able to develop a greater understanding of differences between foreign and Chinese corporate culture and how these can be managed. This is proving useful for companies as they look to expand their marketing and human resources capabilities by looking for local partners in the Western countries. Through direct acquisition, some firms have acquired well-known western brand names such as IBM PC, which otherwise may take decades to build up; they have entered Europe and North America directly, via established distribution channels; they have raised production capacity and global market share immediately; some have acquired access to advanced technology and R&D capability; some to advanced manufacturing capability and managerial skills; some have evaded trade barriers or anti-dumping penalties. Results indicate that Europe, whilst not representing a neighbouring or "home" market, as do markets in South-East Asia could nevertheless be a more approachable target market and, from the Chinese perspective, an interesting market with a potential for higher margins, higher price levels and a more mature market for branding, technology and other resources.

# 6
# MNCs: Competitors or Partners?

## Attractiveness of China

Globalization has caused intense debates on the development possibilities of the developing world, and the impact of foreign direct investment (FDI) on host developing countries is a topic within the fields of regional economics, industrial geography and technological development. The actual interaction between the hosting countries and multi-national corporations (MNCs) tends to result in a dynamic balance to satisfy the desires of both FDI investors and host nations. MNCs have knowledge-based assets, unique resources and core technologies, while local firms usually do not.

The knock-on effects of the activities of multinational firms in hosting developing countries need to be identified. Such effects are most likely to be found in host countries where the operations of foreign multinationals may influence local firms in the MNC's own industry as well as firms in other industries. However, there is no apparent evidence as to the exact nature or magnitude of these effects, although it is suggested that they vary between both countries and industries. In particular, the positive effects of foreign investment are likely to increase with the level of capacity building and competition within the local markets (Blomström & Kokko, 1998). For various reasons, the effects on the home countries of MNCs are often more difficult to identify. Earlier studies suggested that the effects are generally positive, but the increasingly international division of labor within multinationals complicates the analysis. The impact on the home country is likely to depend on the activities which these firms concentrate on at home. It has been an increasing challenge not only for the developing nations to break through boundaries of imitation but also for many MNCs to enhance their competitive advantages through co-evolution with the developing world. Within a high-speed innovation based industry, the information and communication technologies are therefore logically playing a more and more central role in this process. ICT has today become the most globalised industry. With regard to domestic markets, a reduction in government intervention and greater compatibility with global standards seem to have become the prevailing business standards.

Foreign investment has been generally promoted in most of China's industry sectors since China adopted the 'open door' policy in 1978. In just two decades, China has become the country in the world offering the most attractive market prospects for most ICT products and services, thus making ICT a key focus for science and technology (S&T) cooperation between the Western world and China. Until now, most of the world's ICT giants have been eager to have an active presence in China. As far as the regulatory environment is concerned, in the late 1970s foreign ownership was limited to 35%, then raised in 1985 to 49%, and since 1988 majority foreign ownership in joint ventures has been allowed, subject to the state's approval (Tan, 1997). However, preference was mainly given to foreign firms with niche technologies that were not developed by local manufacturers or firms willing to invest in Western China where communication services were poor. Furthermore, foreign firms that have better relationships with various governmental institutions are expected to have greater problem-solving capacity in China's market (Luo, 2002).

Other product development activities tend to be dictated by production, beginning with manufacturing process engineering and then moving up to prototyping and testing, and eventually electrical, mechanical and software engineering. These are in the process of shifting to China from Taiwan and Japan, although R&D, design and development of the latest generation products is still likely to be concentrated in the home countries of the manufacturers.

Although China's economic reform began in the 1980s, the process of liberalization is considered to have been a gradualist approach (Peng, 2003). Many of the economic policies remained quite protective of domestic firms which were established to develop indigenous research and manufacturing capabilities. The government also promoted technology sourcing and procurement from among local suppliers, manufacturers and service providers. As relationships with the government were deemed to be a key asset for gaining market entry, some MNCs established equity joint ventures with influential domestic firms in order to retain control of their own technologies and knowledge in China. WTO agreements allow foreign companies to invest directly in ICT, expanding to China's markets through the normal merger and acquisition approach.

## China strategy of MNCs

MNCs have a straightforward interest in maximizing their own profit opportunities and increasing the security and flexibility of the investment climate in China. Therefore they would favor the removal of any restrictions on FDI by the government of of the hosting country. While each individual foreign firm may prefer special arrangements that permit it to invest while blocking the entry of competing foreign interests, after almost a decade of unsuccessfully pursuing that goal they would perceive a general policy of opening to be in their interests.

Based on the research of MNC subunits in China, Luo (2002) suggests that capability exploitation and capability building are inversely associated with environmental complexity and industrial uncertainty. China's specific business culture impedes capability exploitation but not capability building. While capability exploitation is associated with the use of wholly-owned entry mode, capability building is linked to the joint venture mode. MNCs seeking local market expansion also deploy greater capability exploitation and building than those seeking export market growth. The analysis further suggests that the threats to capability building of environmental hazards are reduced when the joint venture entry mode is used. An appropriate alignment of capability exploitation or building with its identified determinants is found to be associated with high performance.

In the face of strong foreign entrants, Chinese firms originally competed on the basis of price and the advantage of local market knowledge. The WTO has changed the situation to some extent because foreign firms, such as Coca-Cola and Kodak, can enter the Chinese market more easily and capture the same low cost advantages, and they have increasingly developed local market knowledge.

The argument and the philosophy of this book have been inspired by the ever-increasing challenging issues facing Chinese domestic firms. With the rise of the information age, the world today has become increasingly open, online and transparent. Consequently, nations, firms and individuals have become more vulnerable.

The pace of technological change has accelerated and the world is in constant evolution. The rules and implication of competitiveness are changing all the time and the indicators, coverage, influences and different facets of competitiveness need to be redefined. Therefore a study of both the strategy and the relative competitiveness of Western and domestic firms will therefore cover a large number of crucial issues concerned with China's industrial R&D policy, technology and innovation systems, science and technology policy, technology strategy, and the appropriateness and effectiveness of the implementation strategy. We will discuss and reflect on these important issues.

## Operation in China: flourishing manufacturing

Foreign firms have done much better in the hardware market as China builds the world's largest ICT network infrastructure. To develop its information infrastructure, China must invest large amounts of capital and harness new levels of managerial and technological knowledge. So selling equipment to Chinese carriers is not restricted, as long as the local technical specifications are met.

From 1986, China officially encouraged foreign electronics manufacturers to locate their production facilities in China and to partner Chinese firms. The number of such foreign joint ventures in China's electronics industries grew more than 6,000% from 1986 to 1995. While Chinese policies nominally restricted foreign investment in the electronics industry to 50%, the government allowed investments beyond this in Shanghai, Tianjin and Beijing.

During the 1980s, China could only produce out-of-date manual and crossbar central office switches in traditional state-owned firms. The outdated telecommunications network could only supply a very narrow range of services (mainly basic telephony and telex) based on the obsolete switching systems, and the domestic state-owned manufacturers could not supply the necessary digital switching and transmission equipment. The first stored-program control (SPC) switch, F-150, made by a Japanese MNC, was installed in Southern China in 1982. Other MNCs with advanced products and process technologies penetrated the Chinese market quickly. The 1980s and the beginning of the 1990s therefore saw market domination by MNCs' SPC systems. By facilitating the building of China's telecommunications infrastructure, they made huge profits, while the local manufacturers with poor technological capability did not know how to compete (Shen, 1999).

Alcatel (France), Siemens (Germany), Nokia (Finland), Motorola and Ericsson have all had joint ventures making equipment such as switches for fixed-line networks and equipment for mobile networks. All these firms, together with the likes of Samsung and LG of South Korea, have also sold vast numbers of mobile handsets in China (foreign players controlled over 2/3 of China's handset market in 2007). Nokia also accounts for one-third of China's handset exports. As a result, China has become a major revenue base for foreign telecoms companies. Motorola reported a 28% increase in revenue from China (including exports), to US$7.7 billion, in 2004. China became Nokia's second-largest national market in 2004, when the company recorded a 44% increase in revenue from the China market, to US$3.6 billion. At the same time, foreign firms have invested large amounts in China: Motorola's total investment, at US$58.1bn since 1997-2006, makes it one of the largest foreign investors in China (Xinhua Agency, 2006).

The major global vendors have been heavily involved in the market since the beginning of the 1990s, although usually through locally based joint ventures. During the period up to 2000, local markets depended more on the different affiliates of MNCs in China. The two European manufacturers, Alcatel and Siemens, have been successful largely because they have managed to transform their local switching manufacturing operations into *de facto* Chinese companies. Siemens has even removed the German parent's name from the company literature of its local subsidiary BISC, and although Alcatel has reclaimed its prestigious Shanghai Bell operations through a recent share buyout, it still enjoys local status under the government administration. On the other hand, China has managed to create three world class domestic manufacturers (Huawei, ZTE and Datang) slowly over time during this period.

Many of the products sold in China are manufactured in China – and the government is keen to see China become an exporter of equipment from these joint ventures. Furthermore, considerable pressure has been placed on foreign manufacturers to ensure that technology transfer occurs, especially in cases where incentives for these joint ventures have been established.

In the telecom sector, until 1996 foreign companies were allowed to produce cellular handsets but not cellular infrastructure equipment in China; in fact, nearly all of the TACS and GSM networks installed before then were imported from foreign countries. From 1996 onwards, the government both allowed and encouraged local firms to enter into joint ventures for both handsets and telecommunications infrastructure. During this period, the Chinese government will no longer restrict the local production of foreign firms in China to a percentage of their exports.

Subsequently, Ericsson, Lucent, Motorola, Nortel and other foreign manufacturers entered into joint ventures to produce cellular equipment. By 2005 China was the single largest producer of PCs and computer equipment in the world.

Since entry to the WTO in 2001, the regulating paradigm of central and local government in China has mainly shifted from entrance restriction to operational intervention, which usually includes activities like component localization, export minimization, environmental protection and financing criteria.

## Operation in China: silent service

Compared with flourishing manufacturing activities established by MNCs, foreign involvement in the information service provider area is a quite different story. Nevertheless, during the whole of the 1990s China imposed some of the world's tightest restrictions on foreign investment in telecommunications services. Foreign business was not allowed to own, operate, or manage telecommunications networks or services in China. In essence, local carriers were protected by the government from foreign competition in exchange for serving as an instrument of national development.

In the telecommunications sector, the only significant crack in the FDI ban did materialize. In 1995, Unicom, the new operator which badly needed capital investment, developed the *Zhong-Zhong-Wai* (Z-Z-W) financing model as a means of circumventing China's ban on foreign direct investment in telecom services. In this model, a Chinese company (*zhong*) licensed to operate a network created or selected an intermediary Chinese company (*zhong*), which in turn established a joint venture with the foreign strategic investor (*wai*). Complex three-way management contracts between the Chinese operator, the joint venture company and the foreign investor combined equipment leasing, royalties, consulting and license fees in a network supply contract. Through the network supply contract, the foreign investor attempted to realize equity-like returns. There are about 44 signed Z-Z-W contracts with Unicom ventures, of which about 20 are active. These indirect financing arrangements have funneled approximately US$1.4 billion into Unicom's business ventures since 1994 (Zita, 1999). Z-Z-W clearly violated the spirit, if not the letter, of the government's FDI ban. Many foreign firms offered up to millions in capital for virtually nothing in return. Nevertheless, Z-Z-W was the only way for foreign strategic investors to establish a position in China's giant telecommunication services market, and it was the most convenient, if not the only, way to meet Unicom's pressing need for start-up capital. Nearly 75% of Unicom's capital investment came from Z-Z-W financing. In fall 1998, new regulations putting an end to the arrangement were published, prompting protests from foreign businesses and their governments (Asia Pacific Telecoms Analyst, 1998). Foreign partners came to realize the complicated arrangements were risky and did not come close to giving them the managerial participation or control they desired (Mueller & Lovelock, 2000).

Other aspiring entrants into the telecom services market, including companies controlled by the army and the former Ministry of Radio, Television and Film, hoped to employ the same method to enter the vast telecommunication market.

Until the beginning of 2002, direct investment and ownership was technically not allowed. This did not mean it did not happen – but only through special dispensation or quasi-legal means. China would not have opened up to foreign investment in telecommunication services without the need to bargain for WTO accession. As part of China's WTO accession agreement, the market progressively opened to foreign involvement during 2007. Value-added services open first, followed by cellular and then fixed telecommunication service. The deals between Chinese carriers and foreign carriers are improving the ability of global carriers such as AT&T to offer their services in China. However, as the stagnant global telecommunications landscape has not improved greatly for several years, global carriers may not be so eager to expand universal services to areas other than the big coastal cities.

## Beyond manufacturing

At the beginning, many MNCs merely considered China as a low-cost manufacturing base. Since the late 1990s, they have also begun to deploy their R&D centres both there and in India. Foreign R&D laboratories in China are not only important vehicles for local market development, but also increasingly important sources of locally developed technology. On the one hand, governments in developing countries are eager to attract R&D to their local economies; on the other hand, developed countries are concerned about losing their competitive advantage due to R&D offshoring. At the same time, intellectual property (IP) protection is a growing concern.

What are the MNC R&D labs actually doing in China? Now the majority of MNC R&D labs are not just providing technical support, product localization, or product development for the local market; rather, they are developing products for the global market. One of the reasons why foreign ICT firms are investing more in R&D in China is to strengthen their competitiveness in relation to local rivals. Although a share of more than 50% of China's domestic handset market for foreign firms might seem high, it is much lower than the 90%plus that overseas companies controlled in the late 1990s.

Appropriating returns is essential to the continuous R&D investment of MNCs. However, returns appropriation is not necessarily realized through formal IP protection institutions such as the patent system. As the growing trend of R&D globalization has evolved to this new stage, characterized by MNCs locating R&D labs in developing countries, it provides a good test bed to further explore more theoretical mechanisms of IP protection. Considering the weak intellectual property rights regimes these developing countries typically have, it is crucial for MNCs to find an effective way to protect their valuable technologies, thus facilitating returns appropriation from their R&D activities in host developing regions. In fact the effective means of IP protection can greatly assist MNCs' location of R&D offshore, in addition to other well-known incentives such as low cost R&D labor and market attraction.

On the evidence of MNC R&D labs in Beijing and Shanghai, R&D is further specialized within MNCs' global R&D network. Furthermore, IP protection and returns appropriation can be realized through such R&D specialization. The key proposition is formulated thus: hierarchical modular R&D structure can be an effective way for MNC R&D labs to protect their intellectual property and thus facilitate returns appropriation in weak IPrights regime developing countries. While "core R&D" is mostly done in developed countries, "peripheral R&D" is conducted in developing countries. The hierarchical modular R&D structure facilitates the global configuration of MNC R&D labs.

FDI usually provides the developing nations with opportunities to obtain access to capital, technologies, management skills and international markets in order to create local employment and to some extent to strengthen the local technological base. However, foreign investors do not have much interest in promoting industrialization in host nations because their priority is typically to further their commercial interests, usually obtaining profits (Wade, 1990). In line with the regulatory environment in China, the MNCs usually have to setup production lines with local partners and the knock-on effect in terms of tacit knowledge like process, maintenance, and related software design is then triggered.

With R&D centres in Shanghai, Guangzhou and Tianjin, Motorola has developed many programmes targeting senior and middle level managers from the company's suppliers, strategic partners, state-owned enterprises and customers. Motorola University (MU) provides value-added services, the key one of which is delivering educational technology to China, not only to Motorola's own employees, but also to many of the state-owned universities and enterprises. Since 1998, and in cooperation with the State Development and Reform Commission of China, MU has offered management training courses to more than 4,000 managers from 1,000 state-owned companies in 26 provinces across the country. Now more than ever, China needs more Western-trained managers in order to fulfill the country's WTO entry requirements.

China has many well-trained mechanical and electrical engineers, but most lack the hands-on skills that come with experience. Industrial design is especially weak, and marketing and business skills are very underdeveloped. A large number of engineers are produced each year, but quality varies greatly by university. In comparing cost across countries, the average salary for electronics engineers in all industries in the US is about $80,000, compared to $60,000 in Japan, $20,000 in Taiwan, and under $10,000 in China (Dedrick & Kraemer, 2006). Obviously there are cost advantages to moving engineering to China, but differences in productivity related to education and experience can negate the direct cost differences. It is reported that engineering salaries are rising quickly in China, especially in industry clusters such as the Shanghai/Suzhou area, as multinationals and Taiwanese firms compete with domestic companies for talent. The willingness of multinationals to pay higher salaries gives them access to more experienced engineers and graduates of top universities, but at the same time turnover rates are high.

Because of its inability to meet the demands of economic growth from current indigenous resources, the Chinese telecommunication industry relies on foreign investment in its various forms. This is a short-term measure, but in the long term China seeks the additional benefit of sustainable technology transfer. There are various modes of international activity that could have an effect. Of these, international joint ventures appear to be the preferred vehicle for the recipients in question. The nature of the technology is not a major factor. In fact, it appears that there is a definite relationship between the type of knowledge required and the technical development of the recipients. An important contribution of this research to the efficiency of the Chinese ICT industry has been to analyze the components of knowledge transfer and determine how and why it is being inhibited. Explicit knowledge is being readily transferred; however, it is tacit knowledge that has been neglected. A more systematic approach is required to improve the delivery of tacit knowledge transfer. Knowledge transfer is known to be positively affected by the levels of economic development of the recipients. Given the situation that joint venture is a preferred vehicle for technology transfer to China, it is reasonable to suggest that it would be wise and practical to promote the establishment of joint ventures.

## Embedding in China's innovation system

The internationalization of MNCs' R&D activities often focuses on some minor adaptation and testing of its original products for local markets. Few of them engage in developing new technologies with local firms. In July 1998, Siemens and the Chinese Academy for Telecommunications Technology began to jointly develop the 3G mobile technology standard TD-SCDMA. In 2004, Siemens Mobile and Huawei Technologies formed a joint venture to develop, manufacture and market TD-SCDMA technology.

Involvement in local standardization activities was the starting point for MNCs becoming embedded in China's innovation system. Recognizing the possible prevalence of China's 3G standard might determine their subsequent entry into the collaboration network favoring this standard. Forming business alliances with indigenous partners who have strong government support is an efficient way for MNCs to overcome institutional and market barriers and compete effectively for future 3G contracts. By joining the collaboration network of TD-SCDMA (as we saw in Chapter 4), foreign partners began to strategically engage in the commercialization process. In these key international alliances, each side perceives a strategic complementarily with significant synergy effects, while the Chinese partners retain the positions of leading actors.

## Some remaining challenges

However, MNCs face some difficulties when trying to compete in the host country's market. These difficulties arise both on entry to the Chinese market and even after some time, since they also exist in the domestic market. MNCs face different handicaps in the battle against local and other international competitors: poor supporting infrastructure; fragmented distribution channels; IPR protection; protected trade barriers across provinces.

### Regulatory barriers

Government regulation in the host or home country is the most obvious barrier preventing MNCs from using their superior technological and financial resources in host country markets (Hymer, 1976; Dunning, 1992).

### Information barriers

Information barriers arise from MNCs' relative unfamiliarity with the unique characteristics of the Chinese business environment, including customers' tastes, business customs, supporting industries, the culture and the legal system (Hymer, 1976; Dunning, 1992; Zaheer & Mosakowski, 1997). Unfamiliarity with customers' tastes makes it hard for MNCs to customize their products to meet local market demand. Similarly, MNCs will find it difficult to work with distributors if they are not familiar with Chinese business customs of China. Lack of familiarity with material or parts suppliers will also make it difficult for MNCs to choose the most appropriate products and processes.

### Resource barriers

Barriers can arise from constraints on resources, especially financial, that face MNCs when they try to employ their superior technological resources in a host country. Although it is commonly believed in China that MNCs have the advantage in financial resources, in many cases this is not true. In fact, many MNCs face strong competition, mainly from other MNCs. The result is that many MNCs often have low profit margins and have to operate on tight budgets. On the other hand, local firms may actually enjoy higher profit margins. Accordingly, it might be not easy for MNCs to find the financial resources to invest in a host country, even though they have superior technological resources.

### Coordination barriers

Coordination barriers arise from the complexity of coordinating activities within MNCs, making it difficult for them to transfer superior technological resources from one country to another. Coordinating business units around the world is a complex and costly process for an MNC (Doz, 1986). Freeland (1996) further shows that it is not easy to make a multi-divisional structure effective.

### Commitment barriers

Lastly, commitment barriers come from MNCs' usually low commitment to a host country market. For many MNCs, the home country market is of strategic importance (Studer-Noguez, 2002; Bartlett & Ghoshal, 1989). The home country markets may be the key sources of revenue and profits,and superior technological resources may be developed mainly in the home country. In contrast, because a host country might be of peripheral importance in contributing to revenue and profits, or creating superior technological resources, MNCs might have little commitment to China's market. This is supported by empirical studies (Amsden, 2001; Amsden & Chu, 2003; Gao, 2003). Gao (2003) finds that MNCs in China's telecom equipment industry chose to focus on the high-end market, operate in well-developed big cities, and ignore the less-developed cities and regions. They also chose to focus on transferring superior technological resources developed in their home country, without sufficiently adapting them to meet local market needs.

Low commitment to China's markets makes it hard for MNCs to effectively employ their superior technological resources. For example, in the battle for the WLAN standard, China's WAPI encryption code was only granted to a few Chinese firms, and foreign companies were forced to cooperate with them to get into China's WLAN market. The WAPI implementation method was difficult for foreigners to accept. MNCs in the ICT industry successfully mobilized other manufacturers, industrial associations, congressmen and the US government to form a strong network where different actors firmly stood together to boycott deploying WAPI in China's markets (Gao, 2006).

The biggest competitive threat comes from aggressive local rivals like Haier, Lenovo and TCL which are leaner, more flexible, more cost effective and quicker to adapt. Local competitors are also more competent in the subtle art of *guanxi* (relationship). Well-established open global markets in applied technology, advanced machinery, the latest tools and sophisticated materials and components allow local rivals to simply buy much of the technology they need (for example the latest technology developed in Silicon Valley arrives in China within months). Medium-sized Asian manufacturers from Singapore, Korea, Taiwan, Thailand and Malaysia also intensify competition.

## Ericsson's Chinese journey

### Evolution of Ericsson's Chinese business

As the world's largest supplier of mobile systems and solutions, Ericsson first began selling telephone sets in Shanghai in 1892, and its first sales office in China opened in 1985. The first holding company was established in 1984. With ten joint ventures, four wholly-owned subsidiaries and 26 sales offices, Ericsson has 4,500 employees in China in 2006 about 25% of them in R&D. China has became the largest single national market for Ericsson since 1998. In 2001, Ericsson and

Sony also formed a joint venture for handset development which is very active in China.

## Manufacturing Network Layout

Ericsson's Chinese R&D centre is now its largest in Asia and a primary global production base. Its joint ventures are located in Harbin, Dalian, Chongqin, Beijing (BMC), Shanghai, Nanjin (ENC), Guangzou and Wuhan. In 2002, Ericsson recombined its production layout in China in order to drive down costs and speed up global product launches, and restructured the business of its two major joint ventures in China to avoid internal conflicts and benefit from specialized manufacturing and economies of scale. All the mobile communication system business was moved to ENC and all the handset business to BMC. Inevitably, the R&D divisions of those joint ventures adjusted their research fields accordingly.

## NEC: the hub

Ericsson's largest equipment manufacturer in China is Nanjing Ericsson Panda Communication Company (NEC). NEC, a majority controlled joint venture with Panda Group in which Nanjing Panda, the domestic partner, owns 35%, has become Ericsson's supply chain management centre for the Asia-Pacific region. Nanjing Panda Electronics was set up in September 1992 with the manufacturing facility on TACS system. In March 1993, Ericsson established the production line of its AXE-10 switching system in NEC, beginning the production and sale of Ericsson GSM900/1800MHz mobile systems in 1997. In November 2000, Ericsson and Nanjing Panda Electronics announced an agreement on production of CDMA switching systems and radio base stations. Nanjing Panda Electronics today provides CDMA network installation and commissioning services, logistics and technical field support for CDMA deployments. ENC produces and sells Ericsson GSM900/1800MHz mobile systems, CDMA systems, GPRS systems and AXE10 switching systems. Ericsson NEC will deliver all Ericsson equipment and services for the new contracts. In 2004, the WCDMA base station developed and produced in China has been sold to the European market on a large scale. From 1.24 billion RMB in 1998, ENC's turnover reached 10.8 billion RMB in 2005. Business interests extends from fixed switching and GSM mobile systems, to CDMA mobile systems and WCDMA/3G systems.

Ericsson and ZTE, the local leading firm, jointly announced the signing of a strategic alliance agreement to deliver TD-SCDMA solutions for China in May 2005. Under the agreement, Ericsson and ZTE will commence close technical cooperation in the home-grown TD-SCDMA standard area. Ericsson is well positioned to capture the huge opportunities presented by China's fast-growing 3G mobile market, and further enhance the competitiveness for customers in China

## Nokia in China

Nokia opened its first office in Beijing in 1985. The reasons for Nokia to enter the Chinese market in scale for mobile phones as late as 1995 had to do with the size of the market.

Since the mid-1990s, Nokia has committed to long-term development and preferred partnership in China. With its innovative technology, Nokia has continued to strengthen its market position as a leading supplier of mobile and broadband network systems and mobile phones in China. Nokia has established over twenty offices, eight joint ventures and two R&D centres, with over 5,000 employees in China. Nokia is determined to become China's leading enabler of mobility by providing the solutions for fast time-to-market. In moving into China and when developing its business strategy, Nokia gradually built up specific networks of relationships with locals. Nokia Corp (NOK) relies increasingly on manufacturing capacities with Chinese engineers. Nokia has currently two units in China producing mobile phones. One unit is located in Beijing and the other in Dongguan. Nokia has also seven joint ventures and two product development units in China.

The Beijing Product Creation Centre, which opened in 2003, is one of just four R&D labs for handsets that the Finnish phone maker operates worldwide. The Xingwang (International) Industrial Park launched in 2001 is a typical successful case (Yeung *et al.*, 2006). Xingwang is a mobilephone manufacturing cluster specifically developed by Nokia and the Beijing Development Area (BDA) for Nokia and its major suppliers. The 1999 decision by NCIC to relocate its manufacturing operations to a new location within the BDA stimulated the establishment of the Xingwang Industrial Park.

The Park is a cooperative joint venture between the BDA and NCIC – the BDA provides land and NCIC contributes physical buildings.

Xingwang has become Nokia's global manufacturing base for high-tech products, based on its supply chain, and all the major suppliers in the Xingwang Park are also Nokia's preferred suppliers worldwide.

The main tenant, Beijing Capitel Nokia Mobile Telecommunications. (Nokia-Capitel), is Nokia's flagship joint venture in China. Nokia-Capitel is a very significant investment for both Nokia and China; it is the leading producer of mobile telecommunications equipment in China, one of China's largest foreign joint ventures in the IT sector and Nokia's largest mobile phone production base worldwide. Between 2000 and 2005, Xingwang attracted US$1.2 billion in investment and created 18,760 jobs. In 2004, the sales of Nokia-Capitel and its suppliers (to other assemblers) were RMB$26 billion (US$3.15 billion), around 38% of BDA's total sales (Yeung *et al.*, 2006).

Nokia has announced that it will develop its R&D activities in China in the coming years. This is done in order to provide China and the world with top-tier technological achievement by leveraging China's technology resources. Nokia has co-operated with local partners in numerous key R&D projects within third-generation cellular technology and next-generation Internet applications.

In 2006 Nokia began to construct the Nokia China Campus, its new Chinese headquarters and a world-class innovation hub hosting around 1,500 people.

Nokia and China Putian signed an agreement to set up a joint venture to focus on R&D, manufacturing and sales of 3G network solutions for TD-SCDMA and WCDMA technologies in October 2005. Through this joint venture the two companies will provide 3G products and solutions to their customers. The joint venture is located in Wuhan, the capital city of China's Hubei Province. It will focus on network solutions for the 3G standards TD-SCDMA and WCDMA, as well as providing network construction and optimization services. The total investment in the joint venture is 900 million RMB (approximately 90 million euros). China Putian and Nokia will have 51% and 49% shares respectively in the joint venture. Products of the joint venture will be marketed under the Potevio brand held by China Putian. The joint venture will produce TD-SCDMA and WCDMA systems.

Nokia has started the development of a TD-SCDMA device for China Mobile on Symbian operation system, and plans to launch the product before the end of 2009. Nokia's S60 TD-SCDMA device will enrich the

TD-SCDMA device portfolio for Chinese consumers, and promote the development of TD-SCDMA in China.

Apparently, China will be an important home base for Nokia when serving other markets and developing mobile products.

## IPR issues

Historically, the ICT infrastructure in China has come from the US, Europe and Japan. It is clear that an appropriate intellectual property rights (IPR) framework and strategy will help in attracting multinational firms and easing technology transfer.

Since the 1980s, China has passed a number of laws and regulations covering the major aspects of IPR protection. China has also published a series of relevant rules for the implementation of these laws and regulations and their legal interpretation. In 2001, when China was admitted into the WTO, China made revisions to these laws and regulations and their legal interpretation in order to comply with the WTO's Agreement on Trade-related Aspects of Intellectual Property Rights and other international rules on IPR protection.

To deal with the IPR environmental issues, the multinational firms must have the ability to efficiently transfer, integrate, and further develop knowledge on a global basis. Second, the acquisition of a firm's complementary knowledge developed in other countries is subject to the constraints of geographical distance and appropriate IPR protection in those countries. On the other hand, foreign firms with desirable complementary assets will not involve themselves in domestic-sponsored technology development without the need to gain more legitimacy and bargain for further market accession.

## Future implications for MNCs

China's entry into the WTO has changed the international business landscape in an economy that the world is counting on for growth in the coming years, which presents both opportunities and challenges to the international community. China is increasingly becoming an influential country in all segments of the global electronics industry (Linden, 2003). In the light of competition from China as a manufacturing location for the electronics industry, regional complementarities are vital. China is potentially able to perform all functions of the production processes, regardless of whether they are labour-, capital- or even technology-intensive, within one national territory. This would eliminate the obstacles associated with managing a regional production network across Singapore, Malaysia, and Thailand, countries that have different regulations, despite the ongoing process of regional integration in the Association of South-East Asian Nations (ASEAN) and its free trade area AFTA.

While the growing market in China gives multi-national corporations expanding business opportunities, other environmental and energy factors also make the Chinese market challenging and uncertain. The value of the Chinese currency value has been rising recently. The changes in labor laws and tax regulations have affected firms' profits. The rapidly evolving competitive landscape demands new capabilities of global companies in China. MNCs in China are facing intense competition from many other global companies and local Chinese innovative companies (Wu, Ma *et al.*, 2006). Low cost based manufacturing or outsourcing are no longer adequate to ensure sustainable competitive advantage.

Traditionally, MNCs have operated in a single or small number of projects, often using the low risk entry mode to test the water, and have been located in a major coastal city, often targeting first-tier regional consumers with horizontal core products. The case of Nokia demonstrates that the new locations in China are more value-chain than production oriented. Relocating and configuring home production facilities to China was the priority for most early generation MNCs, as some local joint venture partners failed to deliver what they promised, leaving the MNCs to do it themselves. New generation MNCs are active in building a local supply base, purchasing centre, warehouse centres, distribution networks and service centres. Nowadays, leading MNCs are significantly localizing their applied research, product development, training, management and finance. They also undertake educational investment, committing resources to train or educate local customers, suppliers, distributors and partners. A growing proportion of FDI is now undertaken through wholly-owned green-field investments, acquisitions and franchising. Individual joint ventures may be regrouped or united as a part of an MNC's overall global restructuring, or restructured due to the MNC's need for greater control.

Winning market share or establishing key market positioning in China have become important elements in the global strategy of many multinational firms. To ensure success against competitors from other countries or within China, many foreign firms are leveraging their technological advantages and are bringing to the Chinese market more advanced technologies at an earlier point in their life cycle than has occurred before in any other emerging market country since the end of World War II.

As more multinationals establish significant manufacturing or operational facilities in China, they will have the same opportunities to improve their cost structure. When there are many opportunities for improvement, leading local firms can still compete against MNCs by developing strong manufacturing capability, innovation capability and core technologies. Opportunities for improvement might help local firms narrow the gap in core technology between themselves and MNCs. In these circumstances, local firms can offer not only low-cost, mature products but also advanced and new products, as has been achieved by Founder and other telecom equipment firms in China (Shen, 1999; Zhang, 2000; Gao, 2003).

## Summary

Market opportunities are still enormous in China, but the uncertainties and ambiguities prevalent in the Chinese business environment, in particular in the area of creating competition and strategic flexibility in the Chinese context, are neither well understood nor effectively negotiated by the international community. China's business environment continues to present many significant challenges, particularly in how to manage effective business networks and ensure smooth knowledge transfer, especially in international joint venture projects. The consistency of government policy is still a challenge for these multinationals, especially investment policy, taxation policy, standardization of taxation and stable foreign exchange policy. The Chinese government has maintained strong control over the extent of market participation by ICT MNCs, especially in the communication service and internet sectors. More foreign firms have realized that business ties with domestic state-owned firms are an important asset in order to minimize the liabilities arising from their foreign origins. In addition, the complexities of understanding Chinese philosophy and Chinese management style have led to anxieties and hesitation on the part of many foreign firms.

Many MNCs have built their China centres as regional headquarters to consolidate common functions and integrate various nationwide sub-units, which will improve efficiency by consolidating such functions, alongside manufacturing, as promotion and distribution, new investments and project development, relations with the business community, relations with government, training and personnel management. As we have seen, tacit knowledge of process, maintenance and software design is acquired when MNCs set up production lines with local partners. However, we have found that government intervention still has a limited effect; the in-house technological capability accumulated by latecomer firms is critical in this type of globalized domestic market.

To deal with the potential risks, multinational firms must, first, have the ability to efficiently transfer, integrate, and further develop knowledge on a global basis. Second, the acquisition of a firm's complementary knowledge developed in other countries is subject to the constraints of geographic distance and appropriate IPR protection in those countries. MNCs in China are continuously enhancing their core capabilities while balancing the need for outsourcing and in-sourcing in order to sustain their competitive advantage. The realistic option for MNCs in China is therefore to move towards high premium value goods, services and industries.

# 7
# From Imitation to Innovation: Future Trends

## Introduction

China's ambition of becoming "an innovation-oriented country" by 2020 and "the world's leading science power" by 2050 has attracted world attention. In other words, China's leaders wish to see the country transformed into an innovation-oriented society within a relatively short time. Following intense debate about whether China's strategy – gaining technology by sacrificing its market – has partly failed, Chinese enterprises are becoming less reliant on foreign technology (Li-Hua, 2008). As a matter of fact, technology transfer between developed and developing countries is strategically significant in the building of science and technology capability. China's leaders have made "indigenous innovation" a cornerstone of the country's future development. Many indicators and statistics, such as the number of science and engineering papers that Chinese researchers publish in international journals, the amount of investments made in research and development (R&D) and the number of patents registered, indicate that China's science and technology capacities have been developing quickly.

Nonetheless, China's legacy is that it has currently become second only to the US in gross domestic product (GDP) as expressed in purchasing power parity (PPP). China's remarkable global economic impact shows evidence of outstanding and interesting innovation. How could a small village like Shenzhen become a large city of 10 million people in a mere 28 years? (According to *Xinhua News*, 21 August 2005, Shenzhen had 4.32 million permanent residents and

141

more than 6 million immigrants who make their livings as tempo-
rary workers or babysitters in the city.) How could local Chinese
firms, such as Haier and Lenovo, become world-famous brands in
such a short period? Some observers believe that these remarkable
achievements can only occur in China, as a result of radical economic
reform and the character and entrepreneurial spirit of the Chinese
people. Researchers have drawn interesting comparisons between
American-style management and Chinese-style management. They
observe that self-actualization is at the core of American-style management. For example, it focuses on "management by objectives"
and "management by result". However, Chinese-style management
concentrates on the philosophy of "first self-discipline, then managing people" in accordance with Confucian philosophy. There is no
doubt that Chinese-style management will hold an important position in the management field in the twenty-first century. However,
this does not mean that Western-style management will be replaced
by Chinese-style management (Li-Hua & Khalil, 2006).

Having turned itself into the world's manufacturing powerhouse,
China now aims to be a technologically innovative economy.
Whether or not it will become an innovation-oriented country by
2020 has drawn world attention. The question is hard to answer
but should be of great interest to watch. Success means that China
becomes a global leader and innovator in certain areas of technology.
Failure implies that China continues its dependence on foreign knowledge and technology. Clearly, the task of making China an innovative
society goes beyond the scope of any one industry or one firm and ultimately involves both businesses across the board and public policy.
Moreover, there are too many uncertain variables affecting China's
innovative and economic performance.

We attempt to clarify a few theoretical concepts before we address
in this chapter the crucial elements of China's technology strategy in the ICT sector in the last 30 years. However, as "real core
technologies can not be purchased but can only be achieved by
innovation" (*People's Daily*, 2006), there is a growing need to consolidate technological capacity building by developing an appropriate
implementation strategy through technology transfer to technology innovation. It is clear that the success of Lenovo, Huawei,
Haier and others has endorsed the path from technology transfer
to technology innovation. Technology transfer has assumed great

significance and has been a strategic instrument in creating wealth and prosperity.

## What is technology?

It is necessary to understand what technology is before we discuss technology transfer. Any attempt to define technology seems quite challenging in the face of anthropological diversity. People may have different interpretations according to their background. To refer to "technology" in terms of the Chinese parable of the blind men and the elephant would not be surprising (Li-Hua, 2007). The technology is a wonderful, amazing, always changing bag of tricks that helps human beings to live healthier, happier (or the other way round) and more fulfilling lives. To a scientist, technology is the end product of one's research; to an engineer, technology is a tool or process that can be employed to build better products or solve technical problems; to a lawyer, technology is intellectual property to be protected and guarded; to a business executive, technology may be the most important, yet least understood company asset. Technology is seen as a competitive advantage against rivals. Technology means state power to both developing and developed countries. Technology is regarded as a strategic instrument in the achievement of economic targets and in the creation of wealth and prosperity in developing countries, but is used as an important vehicle for profits in the developed countries. The effective use of technology is perhaps the most important issue faced by both developing and developed countries and will undoubtedly become even more critical in years to come.

The word technology usually conjures up many different images and generally refers to what has been described as the "high-tech" or high technology industries. It has to be understood that limiting technology to high tech industries such as computers, superconductivity, chips, genetic engineering, robotics, magnetic railways and so on focuses excessive attention on what the media consider newsworthy. However, limiting technology to science, engineering and mathematics also loses sight of other supporting technologies. In fact technology includes more than machines, processes and inventions. Traditionally, it might have concentrated more on hardware, but these days more on the software side as well. There are many manifestations of technology; some are very simple while others are very complex.

But what exactly is meant by the term technology? Technology represents the combination of human understanding of natural laws and phenomena accumulated since ancient times to make things that fulfill our needs and desires or that perform certain functions (Karatsu, 1990). In other words, technology has to create things that benefit human beings. Miles (1995) defines technology as the means by which we apply our understanding of the natural world to the solution of practical problems. It is a combination of "hardware" (buildings, plant and equipment) and "software" (skills, knowledge and experience together with suitable organizational and institutional arrangements).

Nevertheless the modern view emphasizes the coherence of technology and knowledge and points out that technology transfer is not achievable without knowledge transfer, as knowledge is key to the overall control of technology (Li-Hua, 2004) Some people even use the term technology synonymously with "know-how". Knowledge is closely related to technology since the use of technology on its own is not sufficient for successful implementation. In the majority of cases, especially in complex technology, knowledge, in particular tacit knowledge, is required for successful international technology transfer.

Technique covers the instruments of labour (machinery and tools), materials and the way they are used by labour in the working process. Both social dynamic (working process) and social contradictions (e.g. between machinery and labour) are inherent in this element of technology, as in each of the sub-concepts.

There are three principal components of knowledge: applied science, skills, and intuition. The weighting between these has changed over time, but in every case an adequate combination of types of knowledge must be present. Knowledge is the key to control over technology as a whole, which can be seen both at micro-level (Taylorism) and at higher levels of social aggregation (technological dependency). However, it is helpful to our understanding that knowledge has recently been classified as explicit knowledge and tacit knowledge. Techniques and knowledge must be organized before they can bring about effective results. Organization is therefore an integral part of technology. It seems natural to include the product in a comprehensive technology concept, not least because in practice, the choice of product often precedes the choice of the technique, knowledge and organization by which it is going to be produced.

## Explicit knowledge and tacit knowledge

Knowledge is increasingly being recognized as a vital organizational resource that gives market leverage and competitive advantage. Polanyi (1967) considered human knowledge by starting from the fact that *we know more than we can tell*. In general, knowledge consists of two components, namely explicit and tacit. While technical knowledge consists of these two components, the more a technology exists in the form of softer, less physical resources, the greater the proportion of tacit knowledge it contains. Tacit knowledge, due to its non-codified nature, has to be transferred through 'personal human interactions'. In the meantime, it has to be recognized that tacit knowledge is the key to delivering the greatest competitive advantage and it is this part that competitors have difficulties in replicating. Tacit knowledge transfer is often intentionally blocked precisely because people understand its significance.

Having clarified the distinctive features of technology and knowledge, and of explicit knowledge and tacit knowledge respectively, it is helpful to review the current debate on why China's technology strategy of getting technology by giving up its market has partly failed. In the last 30 years of economic reform, China has achieved tremendous success and seen the most remarkable period of economic growth in modern times, which is set to continue. There is, however, discussion around the strong sales of foreign brands and strong competition by foreign companies against local firms in the Chinese market, and around the fact that China has not really obtained core technology in the car manufacturing industry. It has to be recognized that this book is not in a position to answer these questions. If we consider that knowledge is a key to overall control of technology, then technology transfer does not take place without knowledge transfer. In terms of technology import or technology transfer contracts, what China has obtained in principle is the "hard" ware, such as machinery, equipment, operations manuals, specifications and drawings. However, not the "soft" side at all, which consists of tacit knowledge, including management expertise and technical "know-how" and "know-why".

## Appropriateness and effectiveness of technology transfer

Technology transfer has been a subject of considerable interest to many groups, such as government policy makers, international funding agencies and business executives, because of the close relationship between technology transfer and economic growth. It has aroused the interest of academic researchers not only from developing countries but also from developed countries as it concerns both the transferee and the transferor. Despite all this attention, however, the concept and mechanisms of technology transfer remain vague, controversial, and inadequately practicable. Technology transfer is shrouded not only in controversy and emotion, but also in considerable confusion, owing to the complexity of technology itself and the multiplicity of channels of its transfer (Li-Hua, 2004). One difficulty lies in determining appropriateness and effectiveness of technology transfer, what to evaluate, what needs to be transferred from the perspective of transferor, what was actually transferred from the perspective of transferee, how to transfer and why, since technology transfer has three main dimensions: transferor, transferee and technology itself.

Technology transfer is a crucial and dynamic factor in social and economic development, which has played a significant role in the construction of China's strong economy. The two words "technology transfer" seem to convey different meanings to different people and different organizations. Technology transfer is defined in the Work Regulations of the United Nations as the "transfer of systematic knowledge for the manufacture of a product or provision of service". The concept of technology transfer is comprehensive, including commercial transactions and non-commercial technical aid. If this transfer involves any factors that are beyond domestic control, the transfer takes on an international aspect and therefore comes under the umbrella of international technology transfer, the content of which covers license agreement, technical services, technical consulting and so on. International technology transfer includes co-operative production, joint venture operations, co-operative projects and project contracting (Li-Hua, 2004).

Technology can be adopted from abroad through technology transfer in different ways. Firstly, a multinational firm may invest in a developing country and introduce the advanced technology into the local economy. Secondly, technology can be imported directly as capital goods or as consumer products, such as advanced telecommunications technology and home computers. Thirdly, technology can be licensed from a patent holder for use in the borrowing country. Fourthly, technology can be engineered by the adopting country and suitably modified by local engineers for domestic production. Finally, technology can be secured through the establishment of international joint venture companies.

As the world celebrates a third millennium, technology assumes great importance in advancing every aspect of human endeavour. Technology transfer assumes even greater importance in the ability of countries, companies and individuals to embrace technological strategies and changes in order to advance their competitive advantages in a global marketplace. There is no doubt that technology transfer leverages economic growth and development in both the developed and developing world. It charts the strategic and operational guidance to economic development not only for developing countries but also for advanced and developed countries. Technology transfer has been one of the main objectives of the government in promoting the establishment of Sino-Foreign joint ventures. A significant number of Chinese ICT firms have employed technology transfer contracts as a strategic instrument in their technological capacity building.

Li-Hua's (2004) research into technology transfer has matured, starting from the early period of emphasis on the technology itself, through general management objectives, to the current state of development, where his interest has centred on the appropriateness and effectiveness of international technology transfer. Knowledge transfer is a crucial element in the process of technology transfer, and the study identifies that without knowledge transfer, technology transfer does not take place. Attention has also been focused on the identification of the features not only of technology transfer but also of knowledge transfer.

There seems something inherent in the technology that determines the effectiveness of transfer. Li-Hua's research supports the view that the nature of the technology is not a major factor. In fact, it is quantity of knowledge transfer that predominantly affects the success of the technology transfer. It further appears that there is a pronounced relationship between the type of knowledge required and the technical development of the recipients. The research showed that in general, explicit knowledge is being readily transferred and could be monitored. However, it is the tacit knowledge that has been neglected. It is clear that there were no systematic channels for tacit knowledge transfer in place. This fact could have an adverse effect on the potential for inward technology transfer. Tacit knowledge has not even been recognized as an important factor and its transfer has been merely reliant on chance encounters (Li-Hua, 2004). Furthermore, his study has clearly pointed out that knowledge transfer is crucial during the process of technology transfer in the implementation of joint venture projects. Without knowledge transfer, technology transfer will not work.

## From imitation to innovation

For latecomer firms and developing countries such as China who lag behind technology frontiers, technological learning is understood to be a necessary measure. It is clear that learning and borrowing is the process by which policy makers or firms' managers acquire the contents of the "black box". Obviously, the knowledge and technology capabilities are transformed into economically and competitively valuable resources that support national growth and prosperity.

Xie and White's (2006) research into the learning process categorizes adoption and minor modification of externally-developed technology as fundamentally *imitative* activities. In contrast, a firm's internal development (whether alone or in partnership) of new technology, resources and capabilities involves what we term *creative* activities. Research indicates that successful imitation may be the basis for more pioneering and creative activities. The two activities require fundamentally different mindsets, behaviors and organizational capabilities, and the challenges of shifting from imitative to creative are not trivial. Xie and White (2006) studied the path and learning process of Chinese firms and classified them into 5 stages as illustrated in Figure 7.1.

### Stage 1

The first stage, 1949–1960, is characterized by a strategic emphasis on industrialization and heavy industry, technology embodied in total production systems and transferred through turnkey plant projects and training abroad, and a reliance on the Soviet Union.

149

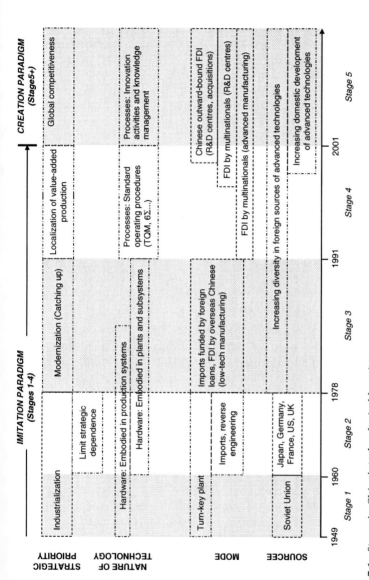

*Figure 7.1* Stages in China's technological learning
*Source:* Xie and White, 2006.

## Stage 2

The second stage, 1960–1978, is characterized by continued strategic emphasis on industrialization and heavy industry, but is marked by a new emphasis on reducing strategic dependence. This change was precipitated by the Sino-Soviet split resulting from the increasingly acrimonious relations between Mao and Kruschev. The shift in China's primary source of technology from the Soviet bloc – essentially a monolithic source – to multiple developed countries is one manifestation of this approach and is a defining feature of Stage 2.

## Stage 3

The third stage, 1978–1991, began at the end of the 1970s and was driven by the technocrats in the Chinese government who recognized that the pace, capacity and effectiveness of China's technological learning was inadequate for China to realize its development objectives. This is signalled by a significant shift in strategic priorities, from increasing production capacity in heavy industry while minimizing strategic dependence, to modernizing China's agriculture, science and technology, industry and military sectors (the Four Modernizations). The Chinese leader, Deng Xiaoping, taking a pragmatic view of China's dependence on foreign sources of technology in order to modernize rapidly, legitimized the opening of new channels with his 1978 Open Policy, a crucial shift from the emphasis on self-reliance and limiting dependency that dominated the previous stage. This shift was reflected in a change in the modes of learning during this period. Perhaps most significant for China's long-term development were the changes in policies that affected human capital development. After more than a decade of chaos and closure, China's education and research system was revived, and a national university entrance examination was held in 1978.

## Stage 4

The fourth stage, 1992–2001, began with a shift of emphasis by the government from modernization itself to localization of value-added activities as a means of modernizing. It was signaled by the point in 1992 when inward FDI exceeded foreign loans and became a major channel for technological learning in China.

### Stage 5 and the creation paradigm

The fifth stage has been from 2001 to date. This period has seen the beginning of China's technological learning, and it represents discontinuous change, with decidedly different imperatives and challenges from the preceding four stages. In this period, the fundamental change is from company and national strategies based on *imitating* technology developed elsewhere, to strategies based on *creating* proprietary and competitively valuable resources and capabilities. Like other major policy developments associated with prior stages, WTO entry signals a major development in the government's strategic objectives, namely to see a growing number of Chinese firms, such as Lenovo, Haier and Huawei, emerging as global competitors. The government has a clear policy of nurturing Chinese firms that will be competitive abroad, as well as domestic firms that can compete successfully against multinationals in China.

## A technology superpower through indigenous innovation?

Before discussing innovation here, maybe the fundamental question "What is innovation?" should be addressed. Freeman (1982) has defined invention as an idea, a sketch or model for a new or improved device, product, process or system. Interestingly, he also notes that inventions may often be patented, but they do not always lead to technical innovation. "Innovation is accomplished only with the first commercial transaction involving the new product, process, system or device" (Freeman, 1982).

Innovation (the successful exploration of new ideas) has to underpin ever higher value-adding products, services and processes. The innovation process depends on a strong foundation of basic science, which is then carried forward to the commercialization of new products and processes. An effective commercialization process depends on several dimensions (Porter *et al.*, 2000). Firstly, there must be a close interface of basic scientists and applied scientists and close collaboration between academic research centres and business enterprises. Secondly, for any products introduced to the new market, the enterprise should be strongly encouraged to make large outlays in research and development (R&D) for intellectual property rights. Thirdly, the economy must be flexible enough to support the rapid adoption and diffusion of new technologies. Most leading developed countries have done well on each of these counts. The government, together with private foundations and philanthropic initiatives, provides vast funding for basic scientific and technological research. Furthermore, the developed countries have developed many innovative methods for linking businesses undertaking applied R&D with universities carrying out basic scientific research. Most importantly, education systems have allowed science departments in universities to participate in private sector R&D undertakings and to own patents for products developed by them. Finally, many developed countries have a remarkably vigorous venture capital system, which can mobilize billions of dollars of financing for the development of and commercialization of new products.

Innovation in the ICT industry has been led from its very beginning by new science findings and engineering breakthroughs. The interactions between understanding nature and technologically fulfilling its potential are driving industry continuously towards a higher level. For example, the transition to the cellular concept of radio signal was achieved through large-scale infrastructure establishment and the development of digital signal exchange switching machinery and various types of technology for individual mobile terminals. The technology is continuously exploiting its potential, pushing back traditional boundaries and eventually creating new demand and markets.

The industry has very successfully taken advantage of the generations of technology and integrating them together in order to orchestrate overall industrial progress. For example, radical innovations in radio transitions are associated with generations of industrial standards. This has proved to be an effective way to coordinate such a complex industry involving many domains of knowledge, a wide range of industrial players and radical technology changes. The development of standards, such as Chinese 3G (TD-SCDMA), is in itself an example of a successful platform integrating fragmented resources and taking a region or a nation to a more advanced level.

Incremental innovations have never been jeopardized by new generations of technology. They mushroom within the scope of a certain generation of standard and improve industry growth. For example, the mobile telecommunication industry has done so much more than any other industry in history to encourage and absorb other complementary technologies and innovations to make itself stronger and stronger, such as batteries and cameras in mobile phones, company specialization in industrial organizations, accessibility and integration with television and the internet.

Traditionally, (R&D) has always been considered the domain of firms in technologically advanced and economically developed countries. The economic strength of a nation will increasingly be determined by the development and ownership of appropriate technology and technology strategies. Those countries which have appropriate and effective IP frameworks and set technology standards for new products will increase their competitiveness. The developing world will face great challenges when they want to enter this domain. Many companies in the developing world are struggling to find a way to transform themselves from imitators to innovators with direct or indirect support from the government and some universities and leading institutes. The mainstream of Western academic research has focused on the early stages of technology transfer, but it has rarely addressed the challenging issues of what happens to companies in developing countries after they receive transferred technology.

High-volume electronics goods such as notebook computers are in fact assembled on labour-intensive production lines; indeed, it is precisely because of the high labour content of such products that China, with its supply of cheap semi-skilled workers, has proved so attractive for manufacturers from overseas. The pricing objective of most Chinese companies seems to be, at least from an outside perspective, maximizing market share, thus assuming that higher sales volumes lead to lower unit costs and higher profits in the long run. Companies in developing countries like China seldom seem to seek to differentiate their products in terms of form, features, performance quality, conformance quality, durability, reliability and style. China has in recent years become a major global producer of information-related equipment and products, including mobile handsets, notebook computers, motherboards, optical disc drives and DSCs. But although many of these products themselves may be considered high-tech, the processes involved in producing them are not. As a big emerging economic power, China is seeking to establish and utilize its growing technological capabilities and market power to develop technical standards approaching technological frontiers and enhance the competitiveness of Chinese firms.

Since its accession to the WTO, China has been significantly expanding its technology research capabilities and production capacity. During the past decade, China's spending on R&D has increased by more than 20% a year. The government is investing heavily in the creation of new technology and the development of standards based around China's IPR and knowledge. It has become one of the world's highest spending countries on R&D activities.

Although China's traditional image as a producer of low-quality and mass-manufactured products still persists, its increasing advancements in ICT technologies and other high-tech sectors are starting to change this image. Based on these impressive advancements, the question may no longer be whether China's technological development will generate important changes in global ICT systems, but rather, when this is likely to happen and in what ways. Some leading indigenous firms like Huawei and Lenovo have not only won the domestic markets but are also trying to be global giants. China's strategic initiatives in core technologies include standards for third-generation mobile telephony (TD-SCDMA), product tracking and remote identification (RFID), digital audio-video coding and decoding (AVS), the formats of audio-video disc players (EVD), and digital home networking and next-generation internet protocols.

## Setting the scene: indigenous innovation

Like any government in an emerging country, China wants to reduce its dependence on foreign technologies and royalties on intellectual property generated externally, and cultivate its own technology-intensive industries and indigenous research capability, moving its economy from cost-driven commodities to technology-driven products.

The issue of knowledge and technology transfer has been an area of great interest for academics, policy makers and industries in both developed and developing countries of the world. Technology transfer has been an area of controversy over the years. In order to reduce poverty, increase world economic strength and reduce the gap between developed and developing countries, the world should focus on knowledge and technology transfer to developing countries. Developing countries should be willing to encourage knowledge and technology transfer as well as local R&D. The transfer of knowledge is not the only economic solution for developing countries; there is also the transfer of R&D. This will empower more innovation in local R&D. Although infrastructure and policy have been a barrier to knowledge and technology transfer in developing countries, one of the main barriers is the IPR (TRIP Agreement) which has hindered the diffusion of technology in the developing countries. There are two schools of thought on intellectual property rights (IPR); one believes IPR in developing countries should be strong to enable countries to attract investors, while the other believes IPR should be weak to allow the diffusion of technology to local industries. If the world economy is truly interested in the development of developing countries, the IPR argument should be properly addressed to ease knowledge and technology diffusion and transfer to those countries. From our research, IPR does create real constraints in the implementation of leapfrogging strategies in the ICT industries of China. These constraints vary widely, depending on the specific technologies and products or services in question, and a major practical problem is assessing whether IPR constraints are likely to apply.

The discontinuity of technological change in IT, the availability of knowledge about key technologies sufficient to create or exploit wider applications, and a broad and competitive market for the producer and user necessary for ICT applications all provide evidence that technological leapfrogging for latecomers is possible. However, there are relatively few ICTs on which IPR has supported effective monopolies or cartels. This is because of computer software's inherent flexibility. This flexibility stems from the many different ways to write computer programs to achieve the same function and thus avoid duplicating a specific "expression" (a specific sequence of computer instructions) in creating software (Steinmuller, 2001).

Assembling the absorptive capacities, complementary industries, and downstream integration capabilities needed for these production activities will play a significant role in the economic growth and development of large developing countries like China. Addressing the challenges in technological capacity building, in 1986 the national government of China launched the National High-Technology Research and Development Programme (the 863 programme jointly proposed by four eminent Chinese scientists) and the National Basic Research Programme (the so-called 973 programme). In 1994, the Ministry of Education formally launched the 211 project, which aims to establish a small number of elite universities to compete with world famous universities. However, it has been recognized that there is a gap between famous Chinese universities and the world class research-led universities of Europe and America.

The appropriateness and effectiveness of the 863, the 973 and the 211 programmes have been discussed on various occasions. These programmes, which have boosted China's overall high-tech development, R&D capacity, socio-economic development and national security, are remarkable in a variety of ways (China MOST website). As a big emerging country, China enjoys the edge with its 1.3 billion populations, the great market this population represents, and the creative potential of scientific and engineering manpower here. The traditional image of China as a producer of low-quality and mass-manufactured products remains, but its increasing advances in some hi-tech sectors especially in information and communication technology (ICT) are changing this image.

As the world enters the information age, and after a long period of imitation and learning from the West, China has realized the significance of "indigenous innovation" (Xie & White, 2006; Simon & Goldman, 1989). In February 2006, China initiated a 15-year medium to long-term plan (MLP) for the development of science and technology, aiming to transform China into an "innovation-oriented society" by 2020 and a world leader in science and technology by 2050. The strategic vision of MLP is to commit China to developing capabilities for indigenous innovation and to leapfrog into the leading position in new science-based industries by the end of the Plan (Cao, Suttmeier & Simon, 2006).

The plan publicizing was noticed both within and outside China. This announcement marks not only China's first long-term plan in the new century but also the first long-term plan China presented since becoming a member of the World Trade Organization (WTO). For the international community, the plan indicates how China aims to strengthen its future economic and technical development, undoubtedly having a profound impact on the rest of the world. The plan warrants careful analysis because it reflects China's ambitions to transform itself into one of the world's most important knowledge bases. Also of importance is that the plan contains an explicit target to reduce China's reliance on foreign research and development as well as to use public procurement to strengthen domestic industry. Additionally, rather than using the word *jihua* (plan), which had been used for previous long-term strategies, the State Council made a point of using the word *guihua,* or long-term programme in science and technology management, distancing the plan from the notion of a traditional "plan economy".

At the enterprise level, 2006 saw "made in China" continuing to arouse curiosity across the world. As a country, China has the opportunity to combine the high technology from the first world and cheap labour and raw material from the third world together. Lenovo purchased the PC department of IBM with US$1.25 billion and moved its headquarters to New York (Li-Hua & Khalil, 2006). Having secured ownership of British MG Rover, Nanjing Automobile, China's oldest carmaker, planned to develop an R&D and technical facility in the UK. Haier Group, Chinese electronic giant based in Qingdao, attempted takeover of Maytag, the US microwave oven and vacuum cleaner conglomerate

In the late 1990s, Chinese policy makers, academic institutions and technology companies increased their commitment to improving external communications with overseas Chinese experts. They sponsored an increasing number of events and programmes in the US, while also inviting overseas Chinese academics and industry representatives to China to attend conferences and other events. Government agencies in China also competed to recruit students to return home to start technology enterprises. Representatives of cabinet-level ministries as well as municipal governments from large cities such as Shanghai and Beijing paid regular visits to Silicon Valley to encourage Chinese technology professionals to return home.

In 2001 the Ministry of Information Industry announced a plan to integrate and consolidate resources in the software industry in hopes of enhancing competitiveness. They have identified 10 National software industrial bases located in Beijing, Shanghai, Dalian, Chengdu, Xi'an, Jinan, Hangzhou, Guangzhou, Changsha, and Nanjing. These ten areas will receive preferential policies including venture capital funding, support services, and assistance with listing on the stock exchange.

## Establishing international competitiveness through innovation

The future of China's technology and innovation will be largely determined by the international competitiveness of its enterprises.

Competitiveness has become a central preoccupation for both advanced and developing countries in an increasingly open and integrated world economy. Despite its acknowledged importance, the concept of competitiveness has often been controversial and misunderstood. There was no accepted definition of competitiveness and no generally accepted theory to explain it. Competitiveness is the fundamental determinant of the level of prosperity a country can sustain (Porter, 2005). To some economists, competitiveness meant a low unit cost of labour adjusted for exchange rates. To firms, competitiveness meant the ability to compete in world markets with a global strategy (Porter, 1990, 1998). The central focus of public policy must be competitiveness, and national leaders must maintain a commitment to competitiveness even in difficult times instead of undermining it through short-term gain. At enterprise level, competitiveness is the ability of a firm or an organization to win consistently over the long term in a competitive environment. Competitive advantage is achieved through five qualities: superiority, inimitability, durability, non-substitutability and appropriability. Core competences or distinctive capabilities are combinations of resources and capabilities unique to a specific organization and generating competitive advantage by creating unique customer value. A core competence must be distinctive, complex, difficult to imitate, durable and adaptable to ensure it is a source of sustained superior performance.

## Creating competitiveness in the ICT sector

Early in 2005, the *Journal of Sino-Foreign Management in China*, through its website and the distribution of questionnaires at its annual conference, conducted an interesting survey among Chinese entrepreneurs on "whom should Chinese enterprises learn from". The result shows that 57.1% (website) and 59.4 % (conference questionnaires) believe that Chinese enterprise should now "move forward on its own way" while only 28.6% and 33% believe that Chinese enterprises "should continue to learn from the West". However, there were different views expressed by three schools of thought in consultancy and academic circles. Chinese business consultants who have education and research experiences and hold Western degrees believed that Chinese management philosophy is essential to Chinese enterprises while Western management knowledge is desirable. Foreign business consultants who work in China believed that Chinese enterprise has not yet been able to establish its own management system within the twenty years since the economic reform. Chinese consultants believed that the prevailing management theory today only benefits and fits well with the Western trans-national enterprises. Therefore, Chinese enterprises should look after themselves and develop indigenous capabilities. These views differed from those of Chinese entrepreneurs and management consultancy circles (Li-Hua & Khalil, 2006).

Competitiveness here may attempt to bring a together a number of complementary concepts aimed at providing a quantified framework for measuring competitiveness and to benchmark the conditions that determine a firm's sustainable level of productivity (Porter, Sachs and Warner, 2000; Lopez-Claros, 2006). The competitiveness of a firm is measured not only in hard and tangible resources, such as land, property, human, financial, technological and legal resources, as in "Description of China's National Team Players" (Nolan, 2001), etc. but also in soft and intangible resources, such as brand, reputation, enterprise culture and leadership, knowledge creation ability, co-ordination, diffusion and sharing, motivation, empowerment, configuration, responsiveness, organizational learning, ability to build new competences and leverage existing competences and so on. The influences on current competitiveness of firms in China can be divided into the following three categories. The first is concerned with the sophistication with which a firm competes. It aims to capture the technology and knowledge, physical capital and managerial expertise which are demonstrated in a company's operating practices and strategies. The second is the quality of a firm's business environment. It benchmarks the quality of the infrastructure, science and technology policy, rules and regulations. The third is concerned with the sophistication of the impact of politics, the economy, culture and legal constraints that economic growth and reform in China have brought. National environments seem more stimulating to advancement and progress than others. Nolan (2001) describes competitive advantage in the epoch of the global big business revolution as core business, brand, R&D, IT expenditure and financial resources.

## The debate on China's technology strategy

Technology strategy in ICT has clearly been the key to building China's technology capacity. What is technology strategy?

A technology strategy has two major purposes. On one hand, it is the translation of the overall strategy of the organization into a coherent set of long term instructions for investment for the sub-organizations that are active in technology development. On the other, it is also the development of technology-based opportunities or options for the organizations to steer future developments, i.e., provide the capacities that enable the organization to shape its future (De Meyer, 2008). To further illustrate what technology strategy is, De Meyer develops (2008) a simplified framework as shown in Figure 7.2.

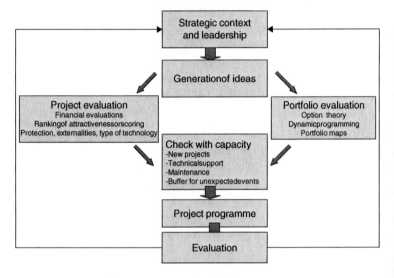

*Figure 7.2*   A simplified description of technology strategy
*Source*: De Meyer, 2008.

In this framework of technology strategy, De Meyer (2008) high-lights the following key elements:

- Creating the strategic context and providing leadership
- Generating fresh ideas
- Evaluating individual projects

- Selecting the portfolio
- Matching the capacity of the technological organization
- Evaluation and revision

Technology strategy is undoubtedly an important but often ignored link in the strategy formulation system. Compared with the position of development and marketing strategy, technology strategy appears to be fragmented and piecemeal. This section addresses the significance of technology strategy in the process of the creation of competitive advantage and highlights the crucial issues concerning technology strategy.

### A vehicle for pursuing generic competitive strategies

Porter (1988), seeking to establish a conceptual link between technological change and the choice of competitive strategy by the individual firm, describes technological strategy as "a vehicle for pursuing generic competitive strategies aiming at fundamentally different types of competitive advantages". He further elaborates that technological strategy must be a broader concept of overall competitive strategy, which is an integrated set of policies in each functional activity of the firm that aims to create a sustainable competitive advantage. Technological strategy is but one element of an overall competitive strategy and thus must be consistent with and reinforced by the actions of other functional departments.

According to Narayanan (2001),to reflect these definitions, a technology strategy should have the following features:

- Technology strategy focuses on the kinds of technologies that a firm selects for acquisition, development, deployment, etc.
- Technology strategy requires commitments surrounding technology selection.
- Technology strategy is not confined to high technology industries. Even a capacity-driven or a customer-driven industry requires a technology strategy. Such strategies may be implicit and may not reflect conscious decisions by executives, but nonetheless they determine the choice of the technical capacities and available product and process platforms of the firms. For example, a banking firm or a hotel in a service industry may decide to invest in information

and communication technology (ICT) as a way of communicating and interfacing with their customers.
• Technology strategy, particularly nowadays, has to embrace both hardware and software elements.

When considering these features, therefore, there are four major types of technology strategy. These are: technology leadership, niche, technology follower and technology rationalizer.

• Technology leadership strategy consists of establishing and maintaining through technology development, innovation and deployment a pre-eminent position in the competitive domain in all the technologies for a dominant market position. In general, the well developed countries often follow this strategy.
• Niche strategy consists of seeking leadership through focusing on a selected number of critical technologies. Technology innovation and development are selective and oriented towards building technological capacity in order to create competitive advantage. Newly developed countries often follow this technology strategy.
• Follower strategy is often adapted by the developing countries in order to avoid the risk of basic research.
• Technology rationalization involves adequately maintaining a selected set of technologies.

Narayanan (2001) proposes that there are four steps in formulating a technology strategy. The first step consists of diagnosis, understanding the environmental context and the firm's strategic position. The second involves the commitment of resources to certain technology choices. The third is to consider the mode of implementation, intellectual property protection plans and organization for execution of the technology choices. The final step involves the execution of the choices and the implementation of the technology strategy.

### Collaborative arrangement of technology strategy

In this section, we use the term "technology strategy" to describe the strategically important technology choices made by a firm or a state. It is a strategic instrument in achieving sustainable competitive advantage. In today's turbulent business environment, there has been a trend towards collaborative technology strategy arrangements.

A collaborative arrangement involves two or more firms in which the partners wish to engage in technology transfer and to learn from each other technologies, skills and knowledge that are not otherwise available. Partners may be suppliers, customers and even competitors.

One of the major features in the collaborative arrangement is the strategic review of knowledge transfer. Collaborative arrangements are often undertaken for strategic reasons. Though partners may try to avoid competition in their day-to-day operations, many technology-related collaborative arrangements are in fact between competitors. Let us consider the case of Shanghai Automobile. The factory was once the flagship of China's car manufacturing industry and the first car was produced there in 1958. In 1991, during the early years of China's economic reform, the first joint venture was established between Shanghai Automobile and Volkswagen, which to some extent took a leading role in China's car industry. The close and successful technology collaboration between these strategic partners has brought the company into the top 500 in the world. However, when Shanghai Automobile wanted to create its own brand, intending to acquire core technology from its German partner, it was rejected by Volkswagen. This clearly indicates that Shanghai Automobile and Volkswagen are pursuing different technology strategies.

The cooperation on the Maglev Railway in Shanghai between China and Germany is another case of collaborative technology strategy arrangement. In 2003, German magnetic train technology achieved the fastest recorded speed (500 kilometers per hour) on the first magnetic railway in the world. Known as the Maglev (magnetic levitation), China's flagship transport system takes eight minutes to hurtle along a 28.5 kilometer track through the paddyfields surrounding Shanghai's Pudong International Airport. This journey normally takes up to one hour by car. The result, as regards technology strategy, is that Germany has been credited with the successful Maglev technology through collaboration, while China has sorted out its transportation problem from Shanghai Longyang Station to Pudong International Airport. This is a win – win solution. Furthermore, the Chinese government is currently considering an extension into the city and possibly beyond, to the neighbouring city of Hangzhou, in time for Shanghai's hosting of World Expo in 2010. Maglev now has admirers across the world as a result of German technology being transferred to China, and Maglev is being considered by Germany for an airport link in Munich. The

US government is also evaluating Maglev schemes. More realistically, the UK government plans to build a Maglev from London to Scotland, which will cost at least £16bn (Li-Hua, 2008).

## No technology strategy without risk

It is clear that technology strategy needs to be tailored to the overall strategy of the organization, and this requires a clear vision to be defined by the leadership of the organization as well the creation of an environment where this can be shared by colleagues and collaborators (De Meyer, 2008). There is no technology strategy without risk. Taking risks requires people to commit themselves. Technology strategies without technological leaders who are willing to take risks are just documents. All these suggestions are universal in the sense that they apply to firms all over the world. But, as we have seen, there are some particular opportunities and challenges for Chinese firms.

De Meyer (2008) advises Chinese firms that the information (whether tacit or codified) that they can obtain from the emerging middle-class consumer about innovative ideas that are unique to the Chinese market and may have global appeal, represents their greatest opportunity. But the first major challenge is that this information is difficult to capture due to ineffective market research, and perhaps due to a reluctance on the part of consumers to reveal their preferences. The second big challenge is the problem of protecting intellectual property (be it patents, brands or trade secrets) and of appropriating the economic benefits for the innovator. The third challenge and opportunity is in the organisational structure. Implementing a sound technology strategy may be hampered by rather hierarchical organizational structure with, on occasions, undue deference to authority. This enhances neither creativity nor flexibility.

Technologies in themselves do not establish the overall strengths of a country. However, an appropriate and effective technology strategy is a key component and driving force in attaining competitive advantage. A country's strategy is the means by which internal strengths and weaknesses are linked to the opportunities and threats posed by its environment. By integrating proper technology strategy into its overall strategy, a country can develop a well-defined technology policy towards technology development and innovation (De Meyer, 2008). Porter (1988), establishing a conceptual link between technological change and the choice of competitive strategy by the individual firm, describes technological strategy as "a vehicle for pursuing generic competitive strategies aiming at fundamentally different types of competitive advantages".

What kind of technology strategy should China have? Should China try to take on a leadership role in technology strategy? Or should it adopt a follower strategy to avoid the risks and cost of basic research? Are these mega-programs launched by the national government effective in technological capacity building? Many people believe that China's technology strategy has played a significant role in developing its economy and technology capability building, while some critics make the point that the strategy has failed to secure core technology. The example is always cited is China's car manufacturing industry; remarkably, cars manufactured and driven in China are almost all foreign makes, and indigenous Chinese brands are disappearing

It has been claimed that the core technology China has gained from multinational corporations has been disappointingly small. Furthermore, China has become dissatisfied with the relative gains it was accruing from its role in international industry (Cao, Suttmeier & Simon, 2006). The royalties paid to multinational corporations (MNCs) by Chinese firms cut into profit margins that are already tight. It has become apparent that it is important to maintain a balance between indigenous innovation and technology imports while having a strategy to encourage MNC technology.

## The catching-up process in the telecom sector

### Technical cycle theory

The potential opportunities for emerging technologies to catch up in developing countries can be identified from the technology evolutionary perspective. According to technical cycle theory, some turbulent periods of innovation end with the emergence of a dominant design or industry standard, which means a single architecture that establishes dominance in a product class (Anderson & Tushman, 1990; Utterback, 1994). Furthermore, the dominant designs or further codified standards mark the transitions between eras of ferment and eras of incremental change. The dominant designs of large complex products like telecommunication systems are comparable to industry standards, which permit significant system-wide compatibility and integration (Farrell & Saloner, 1985). Tushman and Rosenkopf (1992) posit that dominant designs or industrial standards can be driven by a few influential organizations competing for dominance. In the ICT sector too, the development of dominant designs has a profound impact on the competitive structure of the industry and there is a long and complex path to the establishment.

### The catching up process in the telecoms sector

Domestic telecoms manufacturers achieved initial success in the telecommunication switching market in the late 1990s. The telecommunication switching system is the core equipment supporting the modern telecommunications networks. The following stages can be seen in the development of switch technology: manual switching, crossbar switching, analogue electronic switching and digital switching. Digital switching here refers to stored program control (SPC) systems which enable the telecommunications operators to upgrade network performance and provide varied value-added services. The basic design of current SPC switches dates back to the late 1970s and early 1980s (Chapuis & Joel, 1990).

During the 1980s, the outdated telecommunications network could only supply a very narrow range of services based on the obsolete switching systems and domestic state-owned manufacturers could not supply the necessary digital switching and transmission equipment. MNCs' SPC systems facilitated the building of China's telecommunications infrastructure and made huge profits while the local manufacturers with poor technological capability did not know how to compete.

At that time, most MNC local facilities served merely as production centers for the Chinese market, and development work for the local market depended heavily on their headquarters R&D unit. So they responded quite slowly to local demand, leaving room for local firms. In 1984, foreign direct investment (FDI) was first attracted into switch manufacturing through the establishment of China's first large telecommunications joint venture (JV) between Alcatel's branch in Belgium and China. Alcatel's newly-developed S-1240 SPC switch was chosen as the flagship product of the JV and the first product was manufactured in 1987 (Shen, 1999). During this period, Chinese research institutes and firms gradually grasped the engineering and

*Table 7.1* Major multinational corporations in China's SPC switching industry

| Company name | Year of entering China market | R&D staff in telecom sector in China |
|---|---|---|
| Fujitsu | 1982 | 30 |
| Alcatel | 1984 | 2000 |
| Siemens | 1988 | 1100 |
| Ericsson | 1985 | n/a[1] |
| Lucent | 1993 | 500 |
| Nortel | 1994 | 110 |

[1] not available.

*Source*: summarized from Alcatel China, 2003; Ericsson China, 2003; Lucent China, 2003; Nortel Networks China, 2003; Siemens China, 2003; and authors' interviews.

testing technology of the relative circuit, chip and PCB (printed circuit board) and application software technology through cooperation with foreign partners. By accumulating technical capability and operational experience, the indigenous firms began to develop their own primary SPC products.

From 1993 to 1996, Huawei, ZTE and Datang successively rolled out their core SPC products, namely C&C08, ZXJ10 and SP30 switching systems. These firms have complete IPR on these core system products. Starting from a 10% market share in 1992, domestic manufacturers held 43% of China's SPC switch market in 2000. In 2001 the market turnover of SPC switches in China reached $3.5 billion with the rapid growth of the telecommunications network (CCID, 2002). Huawei and ZTE were still leading the race in the Chinese market, grasping more than 50% of the SPC market between them. Eventually the indigenous firms and some surviving JVs came to dominate the local market (see Figure 7.3). The fixed telecommunication service industry really benefited from a highly competitive equipment industry and saw explosive growth. Furthermore, the switch products of Chinese manufacturers have been exported to many developing nations in East Asia, Central Asia, Eastern Europe, and Latin America.

During the 2G era, the indigenous manufacturers followed the technical path and architectures set by the MNCs to develop their systems at a quicker pace. After four years of imitation and redesign, Datang's

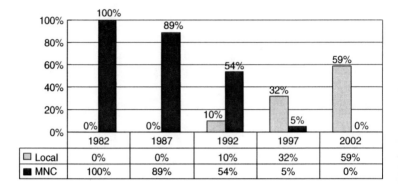

*Figure 7.3*   Rise of indigenous firms in SPC system market in China
*Sources*: MII and CCID.

GSM system finally gained a foothold in the domestic market in 1998. Then Huawei and ZTE, two leading indigenous firms, rolled out their own GSM systems. Also in 1998, Putian developed China's first mobile terminal. In 2000, ZTE and Huawei licensed their core CDMA technology from Qualcomm, rolling out their CDMA system soon afterwards. Table 7.2 depicts the profiles of the leading domestic telecommunications firms.

*Table 7.2*   Leading domestic telecommunication firms and 2G system roll-out

| Company name | Establishment year | GSM system | CDMA system | Sales revenue of firm in 2002 (US$ billion) |
|---|---|---|---|---|
| Huawei | 1988 | 1998 | 2002 | 2.7 |
| ZTE | 1985 | 1998 | 2001 | 1.3 |
| Datang | 1998 | 1998 | | 0.25 |
| Putian | 1980 | 1998 | | 7.3 |

*Sources*: Authors' interview and Fan (2006)

In China, there are three main stages to the catch-up trajectory of telecoms manufacturers: (1) technological monitoring capability, (2) technological assimilation capability, and (3) incremental indigenous technological innovation capability by integrating external knowledge with internal knowledge. Companies that invest in R&D can expect to receive tax incentives and low-interest bank loans as well as the right to depreciate fixed assets such as facilities. At the same time, they have to pay tremendously high patent fees to foreign IPR owners.

## Strategically integrating new product development (NPD) activities

During the SPC catching-up process, Huawei has gradually formulated its product design system as a strategic response to the ever-changing demands of the market. It seems the key factor in successful SPC markets is involvement by local customers in the development and implementation process. Responding to market demand is the responsibility of the product development team (PDT). A cross-functional technical team consisting of engineers from the communications, software, micro-electronics, and mechanics departments, the PDT was established to follow up the entire new product introduction (NPI) process. These unique teams received strong support from senior management and the whole company. When in competition with MNCs, redesign work is critical so that the gap between existing products and local market demand can be captured. The Market Engineering Department (MED), of comprising market experts, was established as a supporting platform to strengthen redesign work among the different PDTs. This department was central to the product development system of Huawei and had no equivalent in MNCs. New ideas were constantly incorporated into the new product development process through customer feedback.

An existing system design can be partially modified for a particular local customer, creating an extension of the product line with an additional feature, function or component. Huawei used the tacit knowledge gained through servicing the local market in the redesign process. The low development cost, which now accounts for a significant portion of the total cost of the SPC switches, enabled Huawei to compete in the domestic market at 60–70% of the MNCs' system prices.

Shortening development cycle times without making concessions on development costs or sacrificing quality has become a key management goal for development (De Meyer, 1991). Huawei began to establish the Integrated Product Development (IPD) system with IBM in 1998 to make the whole product design process more responsive to the market. The cornerstone of IPD is team-based management involving the representation and active participation of all relevant functions during the development process, with the aim of cutting the development cycle time by 40–70% within a year (see Figure 7.2). Huawei set up the integrated portfolio management team (IPMT) to authorize development contracts and launch product development. Engineers from MED and each PDT usually meet and interview business customers and focus groups in the environment where the products will actually be used, so that product development is closely linked with marketing management activities. The market-driven process enables new functions or components to be introduced into the system with minimal production adjustments within the development cycle. Huawei can therefore optimize the development and delivery of successful products and continue to satisfy local customers' new expectations and specifications. A senior R&D manager at Huawei's Beijing R&D centre commented:

> Our rivals are internationally renowned companies with long-term R&D experience. So Huawei must integrate and configure our NPI process according to the practices of the leading experienced MNCs like IBM and then we try to optimize the process by ourselves later to adapt to the ever-changing business environment in China.

Redesign work is closely supported by the production and service sectors within Huawei. A special workshop at headquarters was established for sampling activities. In June 2001, the supply chain management department (SCMD) was established to structure the internal manufacturing network, and its authority has extended to the entire order executing process of approaching, responding to and fulfilling the requirements of the local market. Both Customer-focused and continuous innovation both respond to customers' requirements. As regards maintenance, Huawei promises a rapid service response within 24 hours in the event of any trouble in its switching systems by building a service culture within the firm.

As a result of flexible production and low-cost upgrading services, Huawei obtained most of its contracts from county- to province-level branches of China Telecom in the 1990s. Initially, domestic innovators were not satisfied with simply accomplishing technology development; they wanted to speed it up. In the long run, particular project teams are able to handle more projects if the teams can finish a project faster. However, this also means that at this point, the imitator is only capable of running projects sequentially and is not able to tackle on-going or parallel development projects.

## Attempts to link technology and business strategy

The emergence of a dominant design is central to a period of incremental technological change (Anderson & Tushman,1990; Tushman *et al.*, 1997; Utterback, 1994). During the era of incremental change, the maturation and stabilization of the dominant design makes it more feasible for latecomer firms to focus their limited technical resources on meeting local market needs. The architecture of the product becomes stable, the technical interfaces among the subsystems are standardized and latecomers can access relatively codified knowledge more easily. Furthermore, the product development can build on and integrate the advantages of different systems from different MNCs at the initial stage. Compared with the original development work of MNCs, this strategy often requires less time, less capital, and less human manpower in the commercialization process.

At the beginning, Huawei focused its limited resources on the local niche market, such as countylevel, with its primary cheap product (for example, C&C08A type). It gained both experience and financial resources through the success of the primary product, continuously streamlining its internal redesign process. Most important of all, it began to establish a primary product platform for further local-oriented development. It later redesigned the system and began to penetrate the mainstream sector by virtue of its performance and flexibility. Finally, it began to attack the global incumbents and gain some competitive advantages in the mainstream market with its mature flagship products (for example C&C08B type). A primary framework linking technological and business strategy is developed here, using case study results, as Figure 7.4.

Here we can see the capability building which resulted from the interaction between business and technology strategy implementation. By successfully reflecting the growth of technological capability in their business strategy, local firms can eventually become the

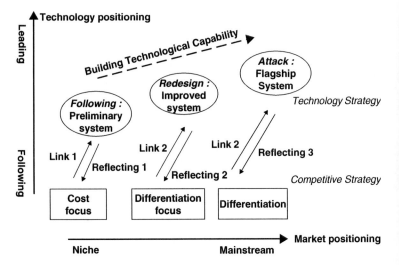

*Figure 7.4*　Building capability by linking business and technology strategy in China

market leaders despite being latecomers in the market. Note that latecomers like Huawei can adopt sequential competitive strategies in different stages as cost focus, differentiation focus and differentiation, and the corresponding technological strategies as following, redesign and attack. The strategic considerations of latecomers in each stage can be identified as the following steps: check the appropriate competitive strategy based on the target market, then check the corresponding technological strategy and establish the link, then reflect the technological capability building in the implementation of a competitive strategy.

## Capturing high-end value from emerging technology

China has tried to distinguish itself from other developing countries by setting the pace in technology standardization. It has set itself the target of becoming an important player in technology standardization and the owner of key technologies. There are some significant examples. China has made efforts to create a national system for high-definition video disc to compete with the Digital Video Disc

(DVD) as a foreign standard, and on 8 July 2004, a national standard called Enhanced Versatile Disc (EVD) was officially published. China has worked hard to promote a domestic technology for interoperability between electronic devices in the home. As a result, in June 2005, China published the Intelligent Grouping and Resource Sharing (IGRS) standard, which was meant to compete with the similar overseas standards developed by the Digital Home Working Group. China has worked on its own Audio and Video Coding Standard (AVS) to compete with the international Moving Pictures Expert Group Standard (MPEG). In software, China has developed its Linux-based office applications to replace the Microsoft system used in government. In wireless technologies, China recently proposed a Wireless LAN Authentication and Privacy Infrastructure (WAPI) standard to compete with the Wi-Fi series (Suttmeier, 2005).

We can examine the dynamics and challenges of such a process through observation of the growth process of China's leading ICT manufacturing firms, with their collaborative innovation capabilities in developing their third generation (3G) systems. Now the indigenous 3G standard is catching up with Western countries. The interests of indigenous firms in developing their own technical standards should be seen as a strategic response to the globalized economy in which standards have become more important for determining the gains from globalized competition. However, in technological evolution the window of opportunity opens for a short period and then shuts forever. Our study of the commercialization progress found that the emerging technology sponsor may rely upon the power of the government for assistance, but it is a power which has limited effect and which therefore must be used carefully in ICT markets. The key determining factors of the commercialization process are still the accessible resources and capabilities of the indigenous leading firms and their partners. It is therefore a great challenge for indigenous Chinese firms, with many defects in their innovation systems, to commercialize standards in a relatively short space of time. In order to meet this challenge, they have to collaborate with more experienced players to further improve their own technological trajectories so as to achieve the dominant designs.

Recently, the uncertainties regarding China's TD-SCDMA technology and its commercial future seem to have lessened. More global players have begun to join the development array and compete against the existing indigenous players in the commercialization process. With close cooperation and a clear division of key tasks, the collaborative R&D network has now expanded from a simple alliance to a competent system-building network. China's market size and increasingly capable technical community give it a unique advantage in challenging established technological structures.

The development environment of the emerging 3G technology has improved with government support and some key R&D milestones since 1999. At the beginning, Datang naturally occupied the dominant position with its core technology and government background. However, bureaucratic management has arguably prevented it from competing effectively. Since 2001, Datang has had to network with more global and local partners, combining their competence, sharing resources, distributing risks, and working from incremental improvements right through to the final success.

The continuing interdependence of product design, engineering and manufacturing are critical in complex system development. The relationship between the indigenous sponsors and some MNCs has evolved from collaboration to, finally, interdependence during the development process of the dominant design-based standards. Although in forming R&D alliances with Chinese players the primary strategic motives of foreign partners have been to reduce their exposure to risk arising from market uncertainties, it seems that both sides of each alliance have recently been perceiving a strategic complementarities with significant synergy effects. The main contributions of global firms are development expertise such as end-to-end solution and global integration capability, which are badly needed by indigenous firms. In addition, the localized design and marketing experience of indigenous players in China are also attractive to MNCs. Capabilities enabled by these alliances are being built not only to solve emerging problems in response to changed environments, but also to perfect the system through continuous improvement and an environment which supports reciprocal learning. With the commercialization process and increasing inter-organizational experiences over time, the marginal costs for the incumbent player forming new alliances decreases. Stuart (1998) argues that with increasing common understanding between firms in crowded technological areas, they can evaluate each others' technical knowledge and facilitate knowledge transfer more cost effectively; this can be seen in the chip sector of TD-SCDMA. As a result, a multi-vendor environment essential for the final business success of TD-SCDMA emerged towards the end of 2006. China is seeking to utilize its growing technological capabilities and market power to develop technical standards that will enhance the competitiveness of Chinese firms.

The 3G scene will see more competition among multiple technological standards on a worldwide basis than the 2G scene, except in Europe. Through 3G case studies (see Chapter 4), we explore how latecomer firms can cultivate their innovative capability and finally outperform the big global brand names in the local market by linking effective technology strategy with business strategy. The study is an attempt to highlight the strategic building process of domestic firms' capability in key emerging countries like China. Though market share is a stronger indicator of a firm's technical capability in a technology-intensive industry like telecommunications, it should be pointed out that government support typically has a significant influence on the firm's business activities in major emerging countries like China.

In accordance with the regulatory environment in China, MNCs have to set up production lines with local partners, which has a knock-on effect in terms of tacit knowledge of, for instance, process, maintenance, and related software design. However, we found the effectiveness of the government's intervention is still limited and the in-house technological capability accumulated by latecomer firms has played a key role in their further strategic expansion in such a globalized domestic market.

From our case studies, we found that the incremental change period in particular represents a critical opportunity for local latecomers. They can take full advantage of both the coded technology and its local market knowledge in the product development process. The large domestic markets tend to be heterogeneous enough to support leading indigenous players strategically climbing the staircase of capability building and finishing the systematic conversion of technologies into marketable products for the local market. Furthermore, the technological capability-based strategy cannot simply be classified in terms of differentiation or cost leadership in the business practices of these emerging countries; they combine both. To quickly introduce new product design, latecomer firms must be constantly aware of innovation both in the structural and functional characteristics of their products. They can continually test, debug, modify, and optimize their new designs and the in-depth knowledge about local requirements becomes critical to localizing the product design on the external platform.

As latecomers approach technology frontiers, learning strategies need to change appropriately. After latecomers have gained their initial foothold in the domestic market, R&D and innovation capabilities become vital for maintaining their margins and sustaining their growth. If we study the rise and the fall of China's local handset manufacturers (see Chapter 4), we can identify factors contributing to the turbulent development of China's local handset manufacturers. We also identify that distribution channels can act as a source of competitive advantages for latecomers to compensate for their technology disadvantages at an early stage. Latecomers should use the relatively strong cash flow generated by their initial market success for their long-term efforts in innovative capability building.

## Ambitions for 2020 and beyond

The official title of the plan is "The National Programme 2006–2020 for the Development of Science and Technology in the Medium and Long Term". (At the Fourth National Conference on Science and Technology in January 2006, "to master core technologies in information technology and production technology" became one of the four ultimate goals for China to achieve by 2020.)

Globalization is beginning to affect the international business environment, bringing to the forefront the importance of studying management concepts as to their synergies or differences between West and East. It seems that the science and technology of the developed countries of the West, and now also Japan, dominates and controls the whole world. Most technologically-based products carrying Western and Japanese brands sell all over the world. However Arnold Toynbee (1889–1975) predicted that the country expected to have more influence in the world would not be from Europe, but China. Management of Technology (MOT) in the West concentrates on how Western businesses should operate to gain the competitive edge. Chinese business executives in China seem to be shifting their international business models. Chinese companies are able to take a "cocktail" approach to overseas acquisitions, depending on the overseas entity that is the subject of a takeover (Lee &

Evan-Jones, 2005). According to Ming-Jer Chen, a business professor at the University of Virginia and author of a new book, *Inside Chinese Business,* among the many Chinese companies attempting takeovers, Haier is going to be at or near the centre of what is happening in China's economy. In other words, what it does will have a big impact on foreign companies that are looking to succeed in China. Haier has been identified as a company with a sophisticated approach and energetic leadership. However, the guiding genius behind Haier's success is its chief executive officer, Zhang Ruimin, whose management theories are strongly influenced by ancient Chinese philosophy.

## Challenges

Enterprises are now said to have taken centre stage in R&D in China. Statistically, R&D spending by enterprises has risen over the past decade. It accounted for 69% of China's R&D expenditure in 2005, which is on a par with R&D spending by enterprises in industrialized countries. However, in terms of quality, the R&D capabilities of enterprises in China are weak, and it is unlikely that many Chinese ICT enterprises can develop R&D capabilities in support of novel, science-based technologies in the near future. It has also been an increasing challenge for policy makers in these countries to break through the boundaries of imitation and devise appropriate public policies to build industrial competitiveness based on indigenous technologies.

## Summary

With the rapid rate of technology development and dynamic environments, latecomer companies that in the developing countries are still imitators would find it increasingly difficult to move into the realm of innovation. But as relevant case studies from Korea and China demonstrate, it is still possible to do so in some technology-intensive sectors.

To some extent, the rise of China and other emerging countries will reshape the global science and technology landscape and their activities will significantly influence the policies of government, industrial firms, and universities. We believe that science and technology policy in China will have broader effects and implications for the rest of the world for many years to come. China's development is part of a fundamental shift in the international distribution of knowledge. Other countries would benefit by responding positively and constructively to this development and working to better understanding China's innovation system. China is still on the way to becoming a scientific superpower and the rising multinational R&D centres, the steady return of the country's scientists from the West and the growing pool of graduates from natural sciences and engineering are helping China to realize its future ambitious goal.

Every effort to innovate is inherently risky, as there is always a possibility of failure. This is particularly so for radical innovations in the big developing countries where the technological and market uncertainties are high. A path-creating catching-up like the new 3G system is a sufficiently large leap forward for those indigenous firms and institutes that it cannot be accomplished merely by pushing traditional imitation approaches to their limit. With less predictability in technological performance and high market uncertainties, a path-creating innovation in emerging market contexts is more likely to happen through evolving inter-firm collaboration. This finding may be of interest to managers in large catching-up countries with home market advantages such as India, Brazil, Mexico and Indonesia.

Institutional support appears to have a great impact on the launching or speeding up of indigenous innovation. However, the institutional influences do not actually translate into strategies of profiting from new innovations. Acquisition, control and ownership of both non-market and market-based complementary assets are imperative for intellectual property development and capability building of China's firms and have played an increasingly important role in their further attempts. The efforts that China has made and continues to make toward technological excellence will certainly reap rewards.

# 8
# The Road Ahead

## Introduction

As we have seen, information and communication technologies have the potential to support the development strategy of "leapfrogging", enabling those big emerging countries like China to bypass some of the processes of accumulation of human capabilities and fixed investment, narrowing the gaps in productivity and output with leading industrialized countries. In the global context, China's ICT industry has gone through an arduous process to establish international competitiveness in several key sectors like telecom systems, handsets, PCs and some consumer electronics products, accompanied with explosive growth in the information infrastructure at the national and local levels. On the other hand, science and technology are needed not only to maintain economic growth, but also to boost the nation's international prestige in, for example, successful space exploration. The traditional image of China as a producer of low-quality and mass-manufactured products has been changed dramatically and its increasing advancements in some ICT sectors are trying to change the dominating positions of Western players.

As to the technological drivers, the primary innovation of digitalisation allows various information and media forms to be united in a common format. Generally, technological drivers are leading to a cross-sector information platform. The expansion of traditional information and communications markets companies into the sector of broadband electronic networks can be accompanied by a considerable increase in growth. This convergence will lead to an ultimate industry restructure with new product and service offerings and a new basic value chain structure specific to the resulting information, media and communications market.

China has the largest market for testing the emerging information and communications technology and services. Because of its unique economic and political environment, China has adopted a unique method to transform its telecommunications industry. The telecommunications reform in China has been a success in that the reform has made China's telecommunications sector one of the fastest developing ones in the world (Gao & Lyytinen, 2000). Here, we will reconsider the dynamics and challenges that China is facing in developing its ICT strategy.

## Reconsidering the role of government

National initiatives for the development of information and communications infrastructure have become critical to moving the whole nation into the information age. Several studies have attempted to explore the impact of governmental strategies on technology diffusion and examine how social factors influence the choice of strategies, such as social determinants for public policy in the information society. We have examined how the deep social transition in Chinese society has shaped the formulation and choice of strategy in a set of information and communications reforms. In their efforts to reform their respective telecommunications sectors, different countries have adopted alternative strategies, thus leading to confusing results. The Chinese case helps to illustrate some of the reasons why specific strategies do or do not work.

As we saw in Chapter 3, China's ICT regulation and policy are also subject to the constraints of its institutional mechanism and structure. The real driving forces behind China's ICT industry came not from inside the industry but from the political vision of Chinese central government and the pressures of accession to the World Trade Organization (WTO).

More importantly, to boost the national economy in the face of global competition, the government was eager to invigorate the whole ICT sector and decided to introduce intensive competition mainly among domestic enterprises. The successful experience of other countries acted as a catalyst for promoting China's communication system transformation. It encouraged both potential competitors and society to appeal for a change and forced the state to review monopoly policy in the interests of the nation.

Yet in general China pursues technological innovation with Chinese characteristics. It has established its technology strategy in accordance with the specifics of economic and political reforms and market development and the requirement of advancing technology (Gao, 2005). The government's strong commitment to the ICT industry, manifested in diverse policies, has made China successful in establishing basic e-infrastructure in a short time. Elsewhere in Eastern Asia, Japan and Korea have similarly established a primary promotion framework and systems based on these emerging information and communications technologies. Support from the government and the local departments ensured the rapid growth of e-infrastructure. Furthermore, we found that the role of the government in the evolution process of the e-infrastructure has changed at different stages of development. While the government was directly involved in virtually every aspect of communication network building in the early days, it seems to play a more limited role afterwards; however, it may decide to relinquish some of these responsibilities in the future. The government appears to continue to stimulate the development of information architecture in its chosen directions.

Furthermore, the development of the Chinese telecommunications sector may suggest a different industrialization path for developing countries. While Japan's successful industrialization and the emergence of the four "Asian Dragons" – Hong Kong, Korea, Singapore and Taiwan – are mostly owing to an export-oriented strategy, China's advances are characterized by the leveraging of its huge domestic market and low-cost human resources. The Chinese case has also demonstrated the significance of government industrial policy in promoting the emergence and growth of indigenous service and manufacturing industries. This is due to the strength of the government and the weakness of firms in China and many developing countries.

There is also no doubt that China's ICT industry will continue to grow. The government's large-scale investments in R&D, education and training, and improvements in the physical infrastructure have already contributed greatly to the economy and will increasingly benefit the ICT industry, as will its huge supply of low cost labour.

The governance of infant industries has not always resulted in internationally competitive products or services; indeed the most common result has been those industries opportunistically enjoying local market power within protected markets, rather than technological leapfrogging.

By recognising the public interests that must be served and by aggressively using the e-infrastructure to provide public services, the governments in developing countries can play the key roles of monitor, supporter, sponsor and enabler in such a process. Multiple roles should be played and integrated, and a coherent sense should be kept in the building process.

For over two decades Chinese policy makers have accelerated the introduction of market mechanisms, but the recent spate of reforms means that institutional change is uneven and fragmentary, and that the entrepreneurial, managerial and technical skills required for developing globally competitive firms remain scarce (Saxenian, 2003).

China has experienced substantial increases in telecom-density and sectional productivity – in part driven by fast technological progress in telecommunications. The Chinese government has been unwilling to commit to complete liberalization immediately, preferring instead a gradual reform process encompassing the reorganization of state-owned operators, the introduction of competition and the establishment of relatively independent regulation. The ICT industry reform followed the process of reform nationwide, in which China adopted an "act after trials" policy of transformation in order to prevent social disorder. As the first macro reform move, the state really had no interest in changing the current system, designed for a socialist economy. Instead, it was implemented as a test for future moves, while the ministries retained a tight control on those state-owned enterprises (Ma & Ling, 1998).

## Universal service

China is a conglomeration of markets segmented by economic development, infrastructure, industrial priority, local culture, purchasing power, and sales distribution. As a vast and diversified country, the penetration rate of ICT services in China is still very uneven across the different regions. There has always been great regional variation in China's uneven economic and social development. The standard of living is relatively high in the southern provinces and coastal areas. In fact, people in these areas have benefited the most from China's economic growth and ICT infrastructure. The country's thirty-one provinces, autonomous regions and cities under the direct guidance of the central government are geographically categorized into three zones: the eastern, the central and the western zones. In terms of economic development, the eastern region is the most advanced, followed by the central region and finally by the less developed western region.

China's ICT infrastructure is naturally characterized by disparities between geographical areas, demographics, and firm size. Large cities and advanced coastal provinces enjoy much better infrastructure and many more comprehensive communication users than remote and economically poorer areas. Large enterprises and government agency have bigger IT budgets and better-trained staff than small- and medium-sized private enterprises. Without substantial involvement by the government, however, it is impossible that the growth of the information infrastructure will become a reality in big countries with such great regional diversity as China.

The realization of universal service is a critical goal for the Chinese government in such a large emerging country. Universal service means the provision of quality telecom services at acceptable price levels for all users and areas, including low-income users and remote and other high-cost areas (Yu *et al.*, 2005). For example, XLT, as a low-cost wireless communication tool, can play a critical role in improving universal service and bridging the digital divides within China.

## Leveraging e-commerce for national competitiveness

China has established great manufacturing capacity in PC production, telecommunications equipment, handset, software, and consumer appliances (Dedrick & Kraemer, 2006). On the application side, the widespread proliferation of the internet, as well as the development of B2B and B2C e-commerce, has enabled many more enterprises and consumers to conduct their business worldwide via telecom networks. China is hoping to upgrade its enterprises to world standards through e-commerce and other IT infrastructures since this upgrading will determine whether Chinese enterprises can survive in the global market after China's concessions to the WTO.

Chinese e-business industry has developed at a dramatic speed. The impressive annual growth rates of B2B and B2C transactions in recent years, as well as positive forecasts, are evidence of China's fast progress in the sector. Since 2001, China has been aggressively upgrading its technology infrastructure to enable the diffusion of e-commerce. However, slow network connections coupled with legal and regulatory uncertainty and competition from the telephone monopoly are among the most damaging obstacles to China's future e-commerce development. Despite great market potential, Chinese firms currently remain at the early stage of e-commerce.

## Local players or global stars?

Chinese firms' positioning or re-positioning strategy has become essential in the context of globalization. Clearly defining the firm's mission and identifying the company's strengths and weakness are the foundation for the competence of those latecomers in the dynamic markets. The boundaries and responsibilities help to clarify the value creation and appropriation. At the same time, however, the industrial dynamics also plays critical role. Dynamically monitoring the position and making wisely moving are so critical that directly relate to survival and growth within the globalized competitions. Fortunately, the Chinese national "champion" firms have a huge home base market that gives them a chance to continue honing their skills for future forays into the overseas battlefield. As competition increases in their domestic market, more Chinese companies will consider the Western markets attractive for their products and services. The near future will see the targeting of Western countries and the subsequent internationalization of a number of these companies, which, regardless of their success or failure, will drastically change the existential business conditions for Western counterparts.

A large number of Chinese firms are "going global". After years of hard work, the operation of several leading Chinese firms across different sectors is becoming more and more internationalized. Some of them, such as, Lenovo, Huawei, and Haier, are trying to establish a global operating network placing great importance on being as close as possible to local customers in global markets. Through international expansion including direct acquisition, some firms now own well-known brand names which might otherwise take time of decades to build up; they have entered Europe and North America directly, via established distribution channels; they have gained some production capacity and foreign market share; some have acquired access to advanced technology and R&D capability; some have acquired advanced manufacturing capability and managerial skills; some even evaded trade barriers or anti-dumping penalty. Previous results indicate that Europe could be a more reachable target market to explore, and from a Chinese perspective, could be seen as an attractive market with a potential for higher margins, higher price levels and a more mature market for branding and technology.

## Continuous innovation with Chinese characteristics

China aims high in science and technology and its leaders have made indigenous innovation a cornerstone of the country's future development. Globally however China is still a borrower, not a creator, of technology. China undoubtedly wishes to establish a national innovation system within which new technology and knowledge can be transformed into economic growth and welfare. There has been intense debate on the effect of globalization on re-structuring the world economy, and especially the development possibilities of the developing world. As far as China is concerned, the country's size allows it to pursue many scientific fields simultaneously and compete effectively across many industries and sectors, unlike its Asian neighbours. Consequently, China can become competitive in a number of areas at the same time, provided it can adopt the appropriate strategies.

However, existing innovation processes result from observation of the current practices of Western innovators. But these innovators have not been imitators. All the innovators were inventors with certain technologies that most companies could not gain or grasp. They are only considered to be successful in the market with their newly commercialized technologies. Thus the innovation processes that have been discovered through observing these companies are based on the evolution from inventor to innovator. Since many technological inventors have become market leaders, the possibility of becoming an innovator has been smaller in developing countries. Hence it is hard to find a company that started as an imitator but later became an innovator and real cases of the imitation to innovation process are somewhat difficult to identify. The process from imitation to innovation is different from other processes.

Today China has not yet developed a mature National Innovation System (NIS) that can effectively combine the nation's scientific base with the private sector and instil a climate of creativity within an effective educational system. The essential elements of such a system are nonetheless being constructed today. In the context of China's extraordinary success as a global cost-driven manufacturer, concern has been expressed about China's alleged "techno-nationalism' (Feigenbaum, 2003) and the possibility that China will exploit its market size and other advantages to exercise technological leadership. Given that many developed nations such as the US, Japan and European Union countries have gained strong footholds in the information and communications networks via standards and intellectual property development, here we have examined the new ICT standardization activity emerging in China, seemingly linked to its goal of promoting indigenous technology. For example, as China's currently booming economy indicates, Chinese telecom manufacturing firms could be seen to have actually done rather well from the existence of dominant global technology architectures (Suttmeier & Xiangkui, 2004). Moreover it is far from clear that the new Chinese standards will reverse the global division of Intellectual property.

Analysis of China is, however, extremely difficult, especially as it is growing, changing and adapting so quickly. China's science and technology output and input is growing at a pace that is distancing it from other developing countries and pushing it towards that of more developed nations. The goal of spending 1.5% of GDP on R&D is attainable, and if it continues it will further increase the speed by which China will reach the R&D spending of developed nations (Forster, 2006).

Keeping pace with the rapid pace of technological change and the emerging new global paradigms of the business environment, the local firms will identify the development trajectory and the way in which firms can contribute to capacity building and the creation of competitive advantage in facing the pressing challenges of globalization. It aims to establish the potential indicators of competitiveness by analysing theoretical elements and the microeconomic business environment. Such a development can also be attributed to a fundamental shift in the international distribution of knowledge. It is predicted, therefore, that the rise of China, alongside other emerging countries, will reshape the global "science and technology landscape" and come to have – if it does not already have – a great influence on the policies of the world's governments, industrial firms, and universities.

As the global economy becomes more knowledge and technology driven, China's local firms are expected to be the driving force behind innovation. During this period, both intellectual property rights (IPR) and technological standards should be developed as tools to strengthen the competitiveness of Chinese companies. The rise of China as a potential high technology competitor and important participant in the world's ICT industry has seemingly come as a surprise to many foreign observers. Though China is eager to move from labour-intensive, low technology production to high technology manufacturing, WTO accession also required a significant re-organization and modernization of China's national innovation system.

Aware of future intense competition on the global stage, China's government is eager to build indigenous technological capability. To quote President Hu Jintao: "Science and technology, especially strategic high technology, is increasingly becoming … the focus of competition in comprehensive national strength" (*People's Daily*, 2006a).

Therefore, integration of the absorptive capacities, complementary industries, and downstream integration capabilities needed for the production and technology upgrading will play a significant role in the economic growth and development of developing countries like China.

## Approaching the frontiers of technology and business

Recognizing the significance of keeping up with the rapid development of information technology and innovations in the world, China hopes to effectively integrate digital communications technology by developing its own proprietary technology to stimulate sustainable social-economic development in the future. However, emerging innovation in dominant design or technological platform level is an integrated process across the value chain and is the way for late-coming indigenous enterprises to become radical innovators, which requires an awareness of the innovation paradigm shift. We found it had been an increasing challenge for not only the developing nations to break through boundaries of imitation, but also for many MNCs in big developing countries like China to enhance innovation capability through co-evolution with the indigenous companies.

There is a diversity of business model development in the ICT industry around the world. It will ask the domestic companies in the developing counties to specialize in its capability, skilful at collaborating with complementary partners from home and abroad, and gain whole chain capability enabling a successful business process. Besides related product and process innovations, domestic companies need to adopt more innovative business models during the further evolutions of the industry. It should be noted that the further progress of China's technology strength will depend on the playing out of a complicated set of tensions: between the planned economy and the market; between national priorities and global networks; between the hardware of research infrastructure and the software of culture, skills and creativity. Above all, can China's growing capabilities in science and technology-based innovation be combined with the social, environmental and policy innovations that will be crucial to meeting the challenges of the next decade.

The growth of the ICT sectors in the fastest growing global economy is really impressive. China is still on the long road to becoming a scientific superpower and the rising multinational R&D centres, steady return of the country's scientists from the west and the growing pool of graduates from natural sciences and engineering are helping China to realize its ambitious goals beyond the ICT sectors.

# Bibliography

Amsden, A. (2001) *The Rise of "the Rest": Challenges to the West from Late-industrializing Economies*, Oxford: Oxford University Press.

Amsden, A. and Chu, W.W. (2003) *Beyond Late Development: Upgrading Policies in Taiwan*, Cambridge, MA: The MIT Press.

Anderson, P. and Tushman, M. (1990) 'Technological discontinuities and dominant designs: a cyclical model of technological change', *Administrative Science Quarterly* 35, pp. 604–633.

Aronson, J. (1997) 'Telecom agreement tops expectations', in Hufbauer, G. and Wada, E. (eds), *Unfinished Business: Telecommunications after the Uruguay Round*, Washington DC: Institute for International Economics.

Barnett, W. P., & Carroll, G. R. (1993) 'How institutional constraints affected the organization of early U.S. telephony', *Journal of Law, Economics & Organization*, 9(1): 98–127.

Becky, P. and Loo, Y. (2004) 'Telecommunications reforms in China: towards an analytical framework', *Telecommunications Policy*, 28(9–10): pp. 69–714.

Blomström, M. and Kokko, A. (1998) 'Multinational Corporations and Spillovers', *Journal of Economic Surveys*, 12(2): pp. 1–31.

Brouthers, L. and Xu, K. (2002) 'Product stereotypes strategy and performance satisfaction: the Case of Chinese exporters', *Journal of International Business Studies*, 33(4): 657–77.

Cao, C., Suttmeier, R., and Simon, D. F. (2006) 'China's 15 year science and technology plan', *Physics Today*, December: 38–43, available in http://www.physicstoday.org/

Castells, M. (1996) *The rise of the Network society*. Volume 1 of *The information age: Economy, society and culture*, Oxford: Blackwell.

CCID Consulting (2003) *The Research Report on the Landscape of China Mobile Industry*, Beijing.

CCID Consulting (2005) *The Research Report of XLT market*, Beijing

CCID Consulting (2009) *The Research Report of China's B2C market*, Beijing

Chapuis, R. and Joel, A. (1990) *Electronics, computers and telephone switching*, Amsterdam: North-Holland.

Cheng, J., Tsy, J., and Yu, H. (2002) 'Boom and gloom in the global telecommunications industry', *Technology in Society*.

*China Daily* (2003) '3G: Mobile firms ponder strategies', 23 September.

*China Daily* (2004a) 'Profits top the agenda for Unicom', 5 January.

*China Daily* (2004b) 'China to kick off 3G field tests again' 3 January.

*China Daily* (2008) 'Industry shakeup creates 3 telecom giants', 25 May.

China Software Industry Association (2001) *2000 Annual Report of China Software Industry*, Beijing.

CIPS (2007) *Report of the Patented Technology of Several Key industries*, Beijing: China Intellectual Property Society, Science Publishing.

CNNIC (China Internet Network Information Center) (2003, 2009) *Statistical Survey Report on the Internet Development in China*, Beijing.

Colin, G. (2007) 'Alcatel-Lucent, Datang snare TD-SCDMA deal', *RCR Wireless News*; April, 26(15), 14.

Comber, A. J., Fisher, P. and Wadsworth, R. (2003) 'Actor Network Theory: a suitable framework to understand how land cover mapping projects develop?' *Land Use Policy*, 20, pp. 299–309.

Data Monitor (2006) *Communications Equipment in China Industry Profile*, Data Monitor Report.

Davies, A. (1997) 'Competitive complex product systems: the case of mobile communications' *IPTS Report*, 19(11): 26–31.

De Meyer, A. (2008) 'Technology strategy and China's technology capacity building', *Journal of Technology Management in China* Volume 3, Issue 2.

Dedrick, J. and Kraemer, K. L. (2006) *Impacts of globalization and off shoring onengineering employment in the personal computing industry.* Report for the National Academy of Engineering, Irvine, CA: CRITO.

Dekimpe, M. G., Parker, P. M. and Sarvary, M. (1998) 'Staged Estimation of International Diffusion Models: An Application to Global Cellular Telephone Adoption' *Technological Forecasting and Social Change* 57 (January/February), pp. 105–132.

Dekleva, S. (2003) 'M-business: Economy driver or a mess?', *Communications of the Association for Information Systems*, 13, pp. 113–13.

DigiTimes.com (2007) 'China-based Huawei and ZTE make headway in global telecom market' 9 March.

Doebele, J. (2000), 'B2B for the little guys', *Forbes*, July 24.

Dong, F., Zhang, L. and Duan, F. (2006) 'The story behind the curtain of TD-SCDMA', *IT Times Weekly*.

Doz, Y. (1986) *Strategic Management in Multinational Companies*, Oxford: Pergamon Press.

Dunning, J. H. (1992) *Multinational Enterprises and the Global Economy*, Reading, MA: Addison-Wesley Publishing Company.

Fan, P. (2006) 'Catching up through developing innovation capability: evidence from China's telecom-equipment industry', *Technovation* 26(3): 359–368.

Farrell, J., and Saloner, G. (1985) 'Standardization, compatibility, and innovation,' *Rand Journal of Economics*, 16: 70–83.

Feigenbaum, E. (2003) *China's Techno-Warriors: National Security and Strategic Competition from the Nuclear to the Information Age*, Stanford University Press.

Forbes (2005) *China Telecom to Build Nationwide TD-SCDMA Network*, December 26.

Forster, C. (2006) *China's Secret Weapon: Science Policy and Global Power*, London: Foreign Policy Centre.

Fransman, M. (2002) *Telecoms in the Internet age: from to boom to bust to?* Oxford: Oxford University Press.

Freeman, C. (1982) *The Economics of Industrial Innovation*, London: Pinter.

Freeman, C., Clark, J., and Soete, L. (1982) *Unemployment and Technical Innovation*, London: Pinter.

Gao, P. (2006) 'Knowledge management in a telecommunications consortium: An actor-network perspective', *International Journal of Technology Management*, 36(4): 387–401.

Gao, P. and Lyytinen, K. (2000) 'Telecommunications in transition: The Chinese experience in the international context', in G. Grand (ed.), *Managing Telecommunications and Networking Technologies in the 21st Century: Issues and Trends*, Idea Group Publishing.

Gao, P. and Lyytinen, K. (2005) 'Formulating effective national strategies for market Transformation', *Journal of Information Technology*, 20, pp. 201–210.

Gao, X. (2003) 'Technological capabilities Catching up: Follow the Normal Way or Deviate', Ph.D. Dissertation, MIT Sloan School of Management.

Gruber, H. and Verboven, F. (1999) 'The Diffusion of Mobile Telecommunications Services in the European Union', *CEPR Working Paper*, London.

Gupta, R. (2001) 'India attempts to give a jump-start to its derailed telecommunications liberalization process', in *Proceedings of the 2001 Telecommunications Policy Research Conference (TPRC)*, October 27–29, Alexandria, VA.

Haug, T. (2002) A commentary on standardization practices; lessons from the NMT and GSM mobile telephone standards histories, *Telecommunications Policy*, 26(3–4), pp. 101–107.

Hoskisson, R. E., Eden, L., Lau, C. M., and Wright, M. (2000) 'Strategy in Emerging Economies', *Academy of Management Journal*, 43(3), pp. 249–267.

Hu, J. and Hsu, Y. (2007) 'Effects of China's communication industry policy on domestic cellphone manufacturers', *Technology in Society*, 29, pp. 483–489.

Hu, Q and Wu, X. (2004) 'Lessons from Alibaba.com: government's role in electronic contracting', *Info* (6)5, pp. 298–307.

Huang, S. and Wang, L. (2006) *The Report on New Digital Media Development in China*, Beijing: China Media University Press.

Hughes, T. P. (1987) The evolution of large technological systems, in W. E. Bijker, T. P. Hughes, and T. J. Pinch (eds), *The social construction of technological systems: new directions in the sociology and history of technology* (pp. 51–82), Cambridge: MIT Press.

Hymer, S. (1976) *The International Operations of National Firms: A Study of Direct Foreign Investment*, Cambridge, MA: The MIT Press.

IDC (2003) *The Asia Computer Market Report*.

ITU (2003) *Mobile overtakes fixed: Implications for policy and regulation*. Retrieved 29 October, 2004.

Jansson, H. (2007) *International Business Marketing in Emerging Country Markets. The Third Wave of Internationalisation of Firms*, Cheltenham: Edward Elgar.

Jefferson, G. H. and Rawski, T. G. (1995). 'How industrial reform worked in China: the role of innovation, competition and property rights', in M. Bruno and B. Pleskovic (eds), *Proceedings of the World Bank Annual Conference on Development Economics*, 129–156, Washington, DC: World Bank.

Jelassi, T. and Enders, A. (2005) *Strategies for e-business: Creating value through electronic and mobile commerce*, Englewood Cliffs, NJ: Prentice-Hall.

Ji, Y. (2007) 'Spreadtrum's Balancing Skills' *CEOCIO China*, November.

Kan, K. L. (1999) 'Where to go for Chinese telecommunication industry?', *Posts and Telecommunications Economic Management*, No. 10, pp. 2–8.

Kano, S. (2000) 'Technical innovations standardization and regional comparison:A case study in mobile communications', *Telecommunications Policy*, 24, pp. 305–321.

Karatsu, H. (1990) 'Right Technology: Technology that is needed', *Intersect*, October.

Kim, K. and Leipziger, D. (1993) *Korea: a case of government-led development*, World Bank Report.

Koppenjan, J. and Groenewegen, J. (2005) 'Institutional design for complex technological systems', *International Journal of Technology, Policy and Management*, 5(3), pp. 240–257.

Kraemer, K. and Dedrick, J. (2002) 'Enter the Dragon: China's Computer Industry', *Computer*, vol. 35, no. 2, pp. 28–36.

Lal, D. and Strachan, P. A. (2004). 'Key determinants of environmental change in UK telecommunications: empirical evidence', in *Proceedings of the 15th European Regional Conference of International Telecommunications Society*, 5–7 September, Berlin, Germany.

Lampton, D. (1992) 'A plum for a peach: Bargaining, interest, and bureaucratic politics in China', in K. Lieberthal, and D. Lampton (eds), *Bureaucracy, politics, and decision making in post-Mao China*, Berkeley: University of California Press.

LaPedus, M. (2007) 'China's Spreadtrum acquires Quorum', *EETimes*, 18 November.

Lee, B. and Evan-Jones, M. (2005) China Acquisition Wave Enters Mega Stage, Hong Kong Trade Development Council, Wanchai.

Li, K. and Shi, F. (2006) 'TD-SCDMA license is still unclear', *IT Times Weekly*, Issue 17.

Lieberthal, K. (1992). 'Introduction: The fragmented authoritarianism model and its limitation', in K. Lieberthal, and D. Lampton (eds), *Bureaucracy, politics, and decision making in post-Mao China*, Berkeley: University of California Press.

Light Reading (2005) 'Huawei Picked for BT's 21CN'. April 28.

Li-Hua, R. (2004) *Technology and Knowledge Transfer in China*, The Chinese Economy Series, Aldershot: Ashgate.

Li-Hua, R. (2007) 'What is technology?' Editorial, *Journal of Technology Management in China*, Volume 2(3) ISSN 1746–8779 Emerald Insight.

Li-Hua, R. (2008) 'China's science and technology capacity building: global perspective and challenging issues'. Book Review of 'Innovation with Chinese Characteristics', *Journal of Technology Management in China* Volume 3(1) Emerald Insight.

Li-Hua, R. and Khalil, T. (2006) 'Technology management in China: a global perspective and challenging issues', *Journal of Technology Management in China* Volume 1(1), ISSN 1746-8779 Emerald Insight.

Liu, C. (2008) 'TD-SCDMA alliance expended its team again', *People's Posts and Telecommunications*, July 23.

Lovelock, P. (1996) 'China's telecommunications policy and Hong Kong, 1997: Bargaining positions', *Telecommunications Policy* 20(9), pp. 685–698.

Lovelock, P., Petrazzini, B. and Clark, R. (1997) 'The Golden Projects: China's National Networking Initiative' *Information Infrastructure and Policy*, 5(4): 265–277.

Lu, Q. (2000) *China's Leap into the Information Age: Innovation and Organization in the Computer Industry* Oxford: Oxford University Press.

Luo, Y. (2002) 'Capability Exploitation and Building in a Foreign Market: Implications for Multinational Enterprises', *Organization Science*, 13(1), pp. 48–63.

Lyytinen, K. and Damsgaard, J. (2001) 'What's wrong with the Diffusion of Innovation Theory: The case of a complex and networked technology', *IFIP 8.6. Conference*, Banff, Canada.

Ma, L. and Ling, Z. (1998) *Confrontation: History of Ideological Emancipation in Modern China's* Beijing: Modern China Press.

Meng, W. S. and Yao, C. F. (2000) 'The "Golden Goose" of Chinese mobile industry', *People's Posts and Telecommunications Newspaper*, 4 July.

Merritt, R. (2008) 'A tale of two chip entrepreneurs in China's manufacturing hub', *EE Times*. 8 April.

Meyer, J. and Rowan, B. (1977) 'Institutionalized organizations: Formal structure as myth and ceremony', *American Journal of Sociology*, 83: 340–363.

Mi, Z. (2005) *ZTE, the Methods of Totally Minimizing the Enterprise Risks* Modern China Press: China.

MII (1999) *Communications Development Statistic Communiqué*, Ministry of Information Industry, Peoples' Republic of China.

MII (2006) *Each Village with Telecommunication Action Plan*, Ministry of Information Industry, People's Republic of China.

Miles, D. (1995) *Constructive change, managing international technology transfer*, International Construction Management Series (ILO) 1020–0142, No. 5, International Labour Office, Geneva.

Mintzberg, H. and Waters, J. A. (1985) 'Of strategies deliberate and emergent', *Strategic Management Journal*, Vol. 6, pp. 260–270.

MPT, MII (1994–2002) *Monthly (December) report of each year on Post and Telecommunications Development*, Ministry of Posts and Telecommunications, Ministry of Information Industry, Peoples' Republic of China.

Mueller, M. and Lovelock, P. (2000) 'The WTO and China's ban on foreign investment intelecommunication services: a game-theoretic analysis', *Telecommunications Policy*, 24, pp. 731–759.

Mueller, M. and Tan, Z. (1997) *China in the Information Age: Telecommunications and the Dilemmas of Reform*, Washington, DC/Westport, CT: Center of Strategic and International Studies (CSIS)/Praeger Publishers.

Narayanan, V.K. (2001) *Managing Technology and Innovation for Competitive Advantages*, New York: Prentice-Hall.

NBSC (The National Bureau of Statistics of China) (1992) *Annual Statistic Report 1992*, The National Bureau of Statistics of China.

Noam, E. and Kramer, R. (1994) 'Telecommunications Strategies in the Developed World: a Hundred Flowers Blooming or Old Wine in New Bottles', in Steinfield, C., Bauer, J. and Caby, L. (eds), *Telecommunications in Transition: Polices, Services and Technologies in the European Community*, Thomsand Oaks: Sage.

Nokia Press Release (2001) 'Nokia drives expansion at new world-class, high-tech industrial park in Beijing', December.

Nolan, P. (2001) *China and the global economy*, New York: Palgrave.

North, D. (1990) *Institutions, Institutional Change, and Economic Performance* New York: Norton.

Oliver, C. (1991) 'Strategic responses to institutional processes', *Academy of Management Review*, 16, pp. 145–179.

Parker, P. and Röller, L. (1997) 'Collusive Conduct in Duopolies: Multimarket Contact and Cross-ownership in the Mobile Telephone Industry', *Rand Journal of Economics*, 28, pp. 304–322.

Peng, M. W. (2003) 'Institutional transitions and strategic choices', *Academy of Management Review*, 28(2), pp. 275–296.

*People's Daily* (1997) 'Deepen the reform of the telecommunication industry', 3 January.

*People's Daily* (2001) 'The installation fee for mobile network will be cancelled from today', 1 June.

*People's Daily Online* (2006) 'China outlines strategic tasks for building innovation-oriented society', 9 January.

Petrazzini, B. and Krishnaswamy, G. (1998) 'Socioeconomic Implications of Telecommunications Liberalisation: India in the International Context', *The Information Society*, (14:1), pp. 3–18.

Pienaar, I. (2004) 'Chinese SMS to top 500bn', *ITWeb*, August 30, http://www.itweb.co.za/sections/computing/2004/0408110738.asp?S=Mobile%20and%20Wireless%20Technology&A=MAW&O=FRGN.

Ping, G. and K. Lyytinen (2000) 'Transformation of China's telecommunications sector: a macro perspective' *Telecommunications Policy*, 24, pp. 719–730.

Polanyi, M. (1967) *The Tacit Dimension*, London: Routledge.

Porter, M. E. (1983) The Technological Dimension of Competitive Strategy. In: Rosenbloom, R. S. (ed.) *Research on Technological Innovation, Management and Policy*, Greenwich, CT: JAI Press.

Porter, M. (1998), *The Competitive Advantage of Nations*, London: Macmillan.

Porter, M. (2005) *Building the Microeconomic Foundations of Prosperity: Findings from the Business Competitiveness Index*, The Global Competitiveness Report 2005–2006, World Economic Forum Policies Underpinning rising Prosperity, World Economic Forum, Palgrave Macmillan.

Porter, M.E., Sachs, J. and Warner, A. (2000) *The Global Competitiveness Report 2000*, Oxford: Oxford University press.

Red Herring (2006) 'China's Telco Titan Grows' 13 February, Print Issue.

Rinde, J. (1999) 'Telephony in the year 2005', *Computer Networks*, 31: 157–68.

Rogers, E. (1995) *Diffusion of Innovation*, New York: The Free Press.

Sangwan, S. and L. F. Pau (2005) 'Diffusion of Mobile Terminals in China' *European Management Journal*, 23(6), pp. 674–681.

Saxenian, A. (2003) *Government and guanxi: The Chinese software industry in transition*, Development Research Centre Working Document.

Scott, W. R. (1995) *Institutions and Organizations*. Thousands Oaks: Sage.

Shen, X. (1999) *The Chinese Road To High Technology: A Study of Telecommunication Switching Technology in The Economic Transition* London: Macmillan.

Shirk, S. (1992) 'The political system and the political strategy of economic reform',. in K. Lieberthal and D. Lampton (eds), *Bureaucracy, politics, and decision making in post-Mao China* Berkeley: University of California Press.

SINA (2007) Annul Report, Sina Corporation, Beijing.

SINA (2008) Annul Report, Sina Corporation, Beijing.

Snow, M. (1995) 'The AT&T divestiture: A 10-year retrospective', in D. Lamberton (ed.), *Beyond Competition: The Future of Telecommunications*, Amsterdam: Elsevier Science.

Södermana, S., Jakobsson, A. and Solerc, L. (2008) 'A Quest for Repositioning: The Emerging Internationalization of Chinese Companies', *Asian Business & Management*, 7, pp. 115–142.

Steinmuller, W. E. (2001) 'ICTs and the possibilities of leapfrogging by developing countries', *International Labour Review*, 140(2), pp. 193–210.

Sturt, T. (1998) 'Network positions and propensities to collaborate: an investigation of strategic alliance formation in a high technology industry', *Administrative Science Quarterly*, 43, pp. 668–98.

Suttmeier, R. and Xiangkui, Y. (2004) (National Bureau of Asian Research) *China's Post-WTO technology policy: standards, software, and the changing nature*, National Bureau of Asian Research Report.

Tan, J. (1997) 'Chrysler's international operation: Beijing Jeep Company', in M. A. Hitt, R. D. Ireland, and R. E. Hoskisson (eds), *Strategic Management*, New York: West Publishing.

Tan, Z. A. (2002) 'Product cycle theory and telecommunications industry – foreign direct investment, government policy indigenous manufacturing in China', *Telecommunication Policy*, 26, pp. 17–30.

Thatcher, M. (1999) 'Liberalization in Britain: from Monopoly to Regulation of Competition', in K. Eliassen and M. Sjovaag (eds), *European Telecommunications Liberalization*, London: Routledge.

Tschang, T. and Xue, L. (2003) 'The Chinese Software Industry: A Strategy of Creating Products for the Domestic Market', ADB Institute Working Paper, 15 January.

Tung, R. L. (2005) 'New era, new realities: Musings on a new research agenda... from an old timer', *Asia Pacific Journal of Management*, 22: pp. 143–157.

Trushman, M.L., Anderson, P.C. and O'Reily, C. (1997) Technology cycles, innovation streams, and ambidextrous organizations: organizational renewal through innovation streams and strategic change, in: Trushman, M.L. and Anderson, P.C. (ed), *Managing Strategic Innovation and Change: A Collection of Readings*. New York: Oxford University Press.

Trushman, M. and Rosenkopf, L. (1992) 'On the organizational determinants of technological change: Toward a sociology of technological evolution', in Staw, B., and L. Cummings (ed), *Research in Organizational Behavior*, Greenwich, CT: JAI Press.

Utterback, J. (1994) *Mastering the Dynamics of Innovation*, Boston: Harvard University Press.

von Zedtwitz, M. (2004) 'Managing foreign R&D laboratories in China', *R&D Management* 34(4).

Wade, R. (1990) *Governing the market: Economic theory and the role of government in East Asian industrialization* Princeton, NJ: Princeton University Press.

Wang, F. (2001) 'A great stride towards 3G's future', *Datang Group Newsletter*, April 1.

Wang, T. (2004) 'Deepening the TD-SCDMA commercialization', *Telecommunication Industry Newspaper*, October 28.

Wang, X. (2005) 'TD-SCDMA value chain is more robust with Ericsson's support', *Yankee Group Report*, May 26.

Waverman, L., M. Meschi and Fuss, M. (2005) 'The Impact of Telecoms on Economic Growth in Developing Countries', Vodafone Policy Paper Series, March, London.

Webster, L. (2002) 'Motorola University scores high grades in China', *Asia Times Online*.

Wei, J., Malik, K. and Shou, Y. Y. (2005) 'A Pattern of Enhancing Innovative Knowledge Capabilities: Case Study of a Chinese Telecom Manufacturer', *Technology Analysis and Strategic Management*, 17(3), pp. 355–365.

Welch, L. S. and Luostarinen, R. (1988) 'Internationalization: Evolution of a concept', *Journal of General Management* 34(2), pp. 34–57.

Wright, M. (2000) 'Strategy in Emerging Economies', *Academy of Management Journal*, 43(3), 249–267.

Wu, I., McElvane, R., Dey, A. and Duwadi, K. (2004) 'The impact of competition and technology on telecommunications regulation: call for further research on regulatory procedures and the convergence of wireless, wireline, and cable', *Info*, 6(4), 225–233.

Wu, J. and Yi, Y. (2006) *The World of Huawei (Huawei De Shi Jie)*, Beijing: China Civic Press (in Chinese).

Wu, J. C. (2002) 'Meeting the challenges of global informatization and networking', speech at PTC 2002, Hawaii.

Wu, X. and Ma, R. (2006) 'Innovating to Create Value for the Mass Customers in Developing Countries: New Dimensions of Secondary Innovation', *Technology Management for the Global Future, 2006*. PICMET.

Xie, W. and White, S. (2004) 'Sequential learning in a Chinese spin-off', *R&D Management* 34(4), 407–422.

Xie, W. and White, S.(2006) 'From imitation to creation: the critical yet uncertain transition for Chinese firms', *Journal of Technology Management in China*, Issue 3, Volume 1, 2006, ISSN 1746–8779.

Xu, Y. (2001) 'The impact of the regulatory framework on fixed-mobile interconnection settlements: the case of China and Hong Kong', *Telecommunications Policy*, Vol. 25, pp. 515–532.

Xu, Y and Pitt, D. (2002) *Chinese Telecommunications Policy*, London: Artech House.

Yan, C. (2006) 'TCL turns off TV business in Europe', *EE Times*.

Yeung, H. W.-C., Liu, W. and Dicken, P. (2006) 'Transnational Corporation and the Network Effects of a Local Manufacturing Cluster in Mobile Telecommunications Equipment in China', *World Development* 34(3): 520–40.

Yu, J. (2006) 'Next generation communication technology: opportunity and challenge for China?', *World Review of Science, Technology and Sustainable Development*, 3(4): 316–327.

Yu, J. (2007) 'From path-following to path-creating, some paradigm shifts in China's catching-up', *International Journal of Technology and Globalization*, 3(4): 409–421.

Yu, J. and Fang, X. (2005) 'The strategic roles of government in e-infrastructure development', *International Journal of Electronic Government*, 2(2): 177–87.

Yu, J., Shi, Y. J. and Fang, X. (2006) 'Innovation Diffusion in a Context of Radical Industry Restructuring', *International Journal of Innovation and Learning*, 3(2): 214–26.

Yu, J. and Tan, K. H. (2005) 'The evolution of China's mobile telecommunications industry: Past, present and future', *International Journal of Mobile Communications*, 3(2): 114–26.

Yu, X. H., Chen, G., Chen, M., and Gao, X. (2005) 'Toward Beyond 3G: The FuTURE Project in China, *IEEE Communications Magazine*, January, pp. 70–75.

Yuan, Y., Zhang, J. and Zheng, W. (2004) 'Can e-government help China meet the challenges of joining the World Trade Organization?', *Electronic Government, an International Journal*, 1(1): pp. 77–91.

Zaheer, S., and Mosakowski, E. 'The Dynamics of the Liability of Foreignness: A Global Study of Survival in Financial Services', *Strategic Management Journal*, 18(6): 439–464.

Zhang, A., Zhao, L. and Shu, H. (2007) 'The evolution of investments decision mode in Chinese telecommunication', *Journal of China Universities of Posts and Telecommunications*, 14(1) March: 122–8.

Zhang, B. (2001) 'Assessing the WTO agreements on China's telecommunications regulatory reform and industrial liberalization', *Telecommunications Policy*, 25, pp. 461–83.

Zhang, W. (2000), 'Is he Alibaba's secret? Interview with John Wu', *e21times*, 11 October, available at: http://english1.e21times.com/asp/ppd.asp?r$^1$/$_4$717

Zhao, J., Wang, S. and Huang, W. (2008) 'A study of B2B e-market in China: E-commerce process perspective–Elsevier', *Information & Management*, 45(4), pp. 242–248.

Zhou, Y. (2008) 'Synchronizing Export Orientation with Import Substitution: Creating Competitive Indigenous High-Tech Companies in China', *World Development*, 36(11), pp. 2353–70.

Zhou, K. Z. and Li, C. B. (2007) 'How does strategic orientation matter in Chinese firms'. *Asia Pacific Journal of Management*, 24: 447–66.

Zita, K. (1999) 'Will China embrace competition? Foreign equity in Telecoms hangs in the balance', *Proceedings of the Pacific Telecommunications Council*, Honolulu.

# Index